# NORMA COOK EVERIST

## NELVIN VOS

# WHERE IN THE WORLD ARE YOU?

## Connecting Faith and Daily Life

AN ALBAN INSTITUTE PUBLICATION

Unless otherwise noted, Scriptures are quoted from the New Revised Standard Version of the Bible.

The Publication Program of The Alban Institute is assisted by a grant from Trinity Church, New York City.

Library of Congress Catalog Card Number 95-83894
ISBN #1-56699-167-6

# CONTENTS

PREFACE

This book is about you and me, the people of God in the world—our struggles, needs, and hopes and what is needed for these realities to be connected to God's mission: spiritual growth (deeper down) and mutual accountability (closer with) in order to be the church in the world (further out).

To be the people of God in the world—this is the central theme of the book. Amid the malaise of mainline denominations and the restlessness and search of each of us, the church is desperately attempting to find new programs to revitalize itself. Instead of launching new programs, this book recommends that each of us simply and clearly recognize the faith-lives and ministry of individual people and of congregations and deepen and strengthen the connections already present between faith and life.

In the midst of the joys and struggles of one's daily life, we need to be aware of our particular time and place, exactly where we are in the world. Both as individual Christians and as congregations, the question is: How are we living out our faith commitment in relation to the realities within and around us?

Such an approach has always marked the growth of the church, both in numbers and depth, because evangelism and witness are basically the power of the Gospel in the ordinary experiences of our daily lives. Because God so loved the world, Christians are the fingers and the feet of the body of Christ; we are contemporary disciples who live out our lives of faith for the sake of the world. And we ask each other, "Where in the world are you?"

The church since New Testament times has possessed the truths and teachings to be the lively people of God in the world: the priesthood of believers, vocation, gifts, the ministry of the baptized. The Reformation rediscovered these teachings and articulated them but did not substantially change the understanding of the church as essentially the gathered believers.

In the last forty years, the Christian community has recovered the biblical and Reformation teachings and incorporated the language into its vocabulary so that the ministry of the whole people of God is almost universally acclaimed. Even the language of the definition of the church has changed. The people of God, for example, is the controlling image of *Lumen Gentium*, a significant statement from Vatican II. Another example that emphasizes the church as the people of God engaged in activity in the world is the *Statement of Purpose of the Evangelical Lutheran Church in America* (1987): "The Church is a people created by God in Christ, empowered by the Holy Spirit, called and sent to be a witness to God's creative, redeeming, and sanctifying activity in the world."

But the church and individual Christians have not recognized the revolutionary implications of being the people of God in the world. We challenge Christians, especially congregational leaders, to make the adventurous but risky changes needed to be the people of God in mission in the world.

We see our readers as laypeople who are seeking to find deeper meaning in what they do in their lives, to feel they are understood, heard, and supported, and to discover how mutual accountability before God and with others is not negative but positive. This book is for you—members of the laity—and about how you choose to live your life.

We also see our readers as pastors and congregational leaders who are looking for ways to focus and strengthen their ministry and the congregation's ministry by concentrating on the ministry of God's people in the world. This book is for you and about how you choose to practice the responsibility you have in the church.

We are writing to people who are struggling with their faith in their daily lives, no matter what their particular function and role in the church. Some readers are already committed to connecting their joys and struggles to their faith and finding mutual help from others in their faith communities. Other readers are at the border; their struggles are so pervasive that they are either considering leaving the church or are already outside, wondering if and how they will ever become more connected to the body of Christ. This book may not give the answer to that dilemma, but it is intended to give insight and guidance to face the struggles with honesty and integrity.

Within the congregation itself, all of us admit not all is always well; we are sometimes torn with conflict and overwhelmed by problems. Yet out of the tensions in our daily lives and within our faith communities may come growth nurtured by Christ because it is precisely by being together in ministry that we can be engaged in mission in the world. The congregation is the natural setting for equipping the saints for ministry in the world. Each person within the body of Christ is called to witness to the Gospel, to be in ministry, to be a priest and a disciple. Each person is uniquely gifted and has worth and identity as a child of God. This book is for you because each of us is connected to God and one another.

The book is designed for use by small groups (either clergy or laity or mixed), adult forum classes, and especially by church councils, boards, sessions, or vestries as they reexamine their purpose or plan for the coming year. This book is a vehicle for spiritual growth and a means for congregational renewal as people connect faith and daily life.

We invite the reader to join us in the journey of struggle and growth. Each chapter has reflections incorporated into the text. Although names have been changed, the stories of people and congregations are true. Individual readers are invited to engage in reflection as they interact with our writing. Groups, such as adult forum classes and church councils, may use the questions for discussion. Readers may find writing responses in a notebook or a journal helpful to reflect on how God is working in their lives. It is crucial that each reader reflect on the connections between daily life and faith that nurture spiritual growth.

The two of us authors have worked together regularly over the past twelve years on writing projects and in various responsibilities within the church. We, in our relationship as a clergywoman and as a layman, have attempted to model the mutuality that the book sets forth. We have evoked each other's gifts and grown spiritually and in trust of each other. In the chapters of this book and of our lives, we have affirmed the worth of the other, have struggled through our doubts and hold each other accountable for the work we do together. Our teaching and writing experience and our passion for the ministry of God's people in the world have convinced us that we have something to say that will be challenging and helpful to the Christian community.

We are grateful to our colleagues in this work: William Diehl, John

Graff, Marj Leegard, Paul R. Nelson, Sally Simmel, and our supportive spouses, Beverly Vos and Burton Everist. We are also grateful to those whose gifts of processing words made this book possible: Dorothy Jones of Muhlenberg College and Patricia Schmidt and Karn Severson Carroll of Wartburg Theological Seminary.

We acknowledge with thanks the many students and conference and workshop participants who have shared their stories with us and from whom we have learned so much.

—Norma Cook Everist and Nelvin Vos

# PART 1

# Where in the world are you?

Where in the world are you? In the pace of daily life, we rarely take time to ask or answer that question. But it's an important question because we need to begin where each of us is located, is invested—in the hustle and bustle of daily life.

So we begin this book where each of us is, with four pressure points: commitment, doubt, stress, and power. These four might not be the exact four you would first mention, but they are the ones contemporary Christians living in North America identify again and again. Often these struggles are deep within us as people and as congregations. Such struggles cannot keep us from being the body of Christ, but they can hinder our fully doing what is the essential priority of individual Christians and of the church: to be in mission in the world, to share the great Good News.

Amazingly what you and I may realize is that God is deep at work amid the struggles and hopes and needs. In the cauldron of our daily living with its tensions and joys, we may find that not only do we cope pretty well with what we have to face, but also by the grace of God and the presence of the Holy Spirit, we already have some answers to the dilemmas we encounter.

To explore, to probe our specific experiences, helps us not only to understand ourselves, but also to listen and to pay close attention to the struggles, hopes, and needs of those around us. To listen and care, we need to know where our family, friends, and neighbors are.

So please take some time with the invitations within these chapters to reflect, journal, discuss, and, perhaps, act. The first part of this book will not give definitive answers. It is an opportunity to explore and probe the questions, your own questions about where you are and what that means to you.

# *Longing for Commitment*

Keeping commitments is difficult, whether keeping a promise to meet for lunch at 12:00 (instead of showing up at 12:45), being loyal to a colleague, or being faithful to one's spouse. Commitment seems in short supply, at least commitment that lasts longer than a few weeks, but it is desperately needed. Some of us like to keep things open-ended. Others want the security of long-term promises. Is the difference just a matter of lifestyle? Maybe we simply have differing temperaments? Human beings hunger for commitment yet often find faithfulness elusive, maybe frightening; we may experience relationships as a complicated web of disappointment.

We long for the joy of living in a healthy committed relationship of mutual promise keeping because we have been created for interdependence. We long for commitment; we need to be committed to someone and something. We also want our freedom, of choice, of movement, of time. Does being faithful to you trap me? One partner may say, "I'm too busy; I have too many other commitments to let my life revolve around yours." The other may respond, "I don't have time to wait around for you . . . but I need your presence in my life."

We want to have it both ways, the benefits of being able to rely on someone's commitment to us and the freedom from having our future determined by the needs and desires of others. We would like a relationship without demands, commitment without entrapment. We would like someone to take perfect care of us, but we resent someone having so much influence over us.

But just maybe, at its best, commitment does not have to entrap but can actually free us. Perhaps promise keeping does not need to add to the stress of a time-pressured life, but can relieve not only our loneliness, but also the burden of our responsibilities.


**Reflection**

1.   Who are the people in your life with whom you have made a commitment?
2.   Make a list, or a series of concentric circles, showing the various levels/types of commitments in the arenas of your life. What are you feeling about what you see on that paper? Too many? The wrong ones? Solid, healthy commitments?
3.   Are you feeling supported or abandoned? Challenged or underestimated?


## Sorting Out Our Commitments

The list of commitments we make and try to maintain may be longer than we realize. Or the truly close commitments may be fewer than we think. Some commitments are explicit, verbalized in some way every day as we shuffle schedules and negotiate responsibilities. Others remain in the background, contributing to our sense of well-being, even our identity. Or does their sheer volume only add to the weight of demand? We may find it helpful to sort out the various relationships we have entered and review expectations.

---

### Meet Dave

Dave is a forty-two-year-old, upper-middle-class, corporate executive. He is vice-president of manufacturing for a nationally known business products company. In several areas of his work and personal life, he struggles with commitment.
    Recently Dave's company was bought out by its largest

---

competitor. In the ensuing corporate reshuffling and downsizing, Dave has been charged with the task of firing several blue- and white-collar workers, many with whom he came up through the professional ranks. Dave now struggles with where his loyalties lie: with the new, controlling company or with the friends with whom he has worked for twelve years? To which group does he belong? The decisions he must make over the next few months will affect many people's lives.

In regard to his personal life, Dave says, "I work sixty to seventy hours a week. I get up, go to work, deal with all the _____, and then go home to eat and sleep, just to do it all over again. Yeah, I make good money. We bought our new house. We have two new cars, but is that all there is to life?" He thought that perhaps the church would provide the missing dimension to his life. Unfortunately he doesn't feel as though he really belongs to the church he attends. The sermons about salvation, righteousness, and sin just don't seem to connect.

Right now it seems that home and family are the best things on which to ground his life. That's his basic commitment. He wonders, *Is that enough?*

1. What in Dave's story relates to your own?

2. What happens to us when we find it impossible to keep all of our commitments?

We need to know we are created for mutuality, not for inappropriate dependency. We are called to healthy relationships. When we expect the other will perfectly care for us, we will be disappointed because no one person can be our god. Nor can we be the ultimate provider, healer, protector for a spouse, friend, or child. We need to sort out expectations. How can we know which commitments will be life-giving? We know what it feels like to be let down. We also know the joy of invigorating partnerships. Such relationships are a rare gift; they can be fostered.

Spiritually healthy people make healthy commitments and have the fortitude and wisdom to help them grow. Even so, human beings won't keep promises perfectly. We won't always love each other wisely or honor each other carefully. Being spiritually healthy means trusting in God's care and strength. Then we are more able to receive the other person as a gift, not as a person we need to save or as someone we expect will save us. When you think my commitment to you means you can depend on me for every physical and emotional need, I'm bound to let you down. When you try to love me completely and protect me from everything, I grow dependent in unhealthy ways. But when I trust God to be God, I am no longer so dependent on you. Likewise I'm then able to make healthy commitments. God can shape us for relationships of healthy interdependence.

We cannot live without commitments. The question is not if we will make them but how. Our past disappointments may cause us to be wary. We vow we will never get into long-term friendships or partnerships again. When we suffer rejection or abandonment or betrayal, we wonder whom we can trust. The one to whom I am faithful and who is faithful to me may die. Neither of us can control that. Such pain seems too much to bear. Someone I've depended on may leave me for other interests or simply forget about me. Despite the risks, we will make commitments, for we cannot live without doing so, and often they will be a life-giving joy.

## Probing Further

1.  Are some of your commitments inappropriately weighted so that one does most of the promise keeping and one most of the promise breaking?
2.  What do you believe to be the characteristics of a healthy mutual commitment?
3.  Compare your list with the list of someone with whom you have a commitment. Share expectations and disappointments. Discuss ways to achieve a healthy, balanced relationship.

## Can we maintain commitments in a free, mobile society?

We are created for relationship and interdependence and through that interdependence our common life is sustained. That reality involves myriads of connections with some people we will never meet personally, such as the one who grows the apples we eat or the one who manages the investments made by our insurance company. We all have some responsibility for the commonweal. In some ways, our honesty, lack of greed, and concern for justice are ways of keeping commitments in the local and global communities of which we are all a part. Even so, society itself will not make us completely secure, nor will my hard work *per se* save the world. And yet we are created to live in healthy mutuality.

But mobility can complicate our mutuality. Sustaining a commitment is not easy in a mobile society. The number of people we meet, the number of choices we have, is enriching to a point. But the number of people we meet calls for more commitments than we can seemingly make. Overabundance and unending choice fatigues, confuses, and eventually debilitates us. Being able to go anywhere and do anything frees us, but can also overwhelm and depress us.

Mobility and multiple choice may seem like freedom, but is it? Some people believe the American way of life—free elections, being free from unquestioned allegiance to a sovereign, freedom of assembly and association—guarantees freedom to do whatever we want. But freedom without commitment leaves us empty. Always and only doing "whatever I want" finally leads me nowhere. One definition of oppressive poverty is lack of choices, but too much free choice feels like a new kind of bondage. Increasingly we as a people suffer from a bondage of excessive free choice. If we are bound to no one, no community, we are bound to self. And in our overemphasis on freedom for the individual, we suffer the absence of communities committed to one another.

Freedom and commitment are not opposites. We are freed from enforced choice, so that we can make healthy choices. We are freed from mandatory allegiance, so that we can voluntarily join and maintain membership in associations where we can meaningfully serve. We must be liberated from abusive relationships so that we can willingly shape solid partnerships. Freedom *from* is freedom *for*.

Take Jan. She's moved ten times in the past five years and aches to settle into one place and really unpack. Yet she's not uncomfortable with the decisions that led to those moves. She makes a point of keeping connected with a few sustaining relationships; her high phone bill is worth it.

Take Fred. He's had a hard time discovering what he wants, where he's going. Maybe he never will find the perfect job in the perfect location, but he decided to join a faith community. He finally feels grounded and connected.

Take Sarah. She made an early commitment to a marriage relationship that turned abusive. For months she thought she couldn't "get out," and she felt guilty for wanting to. A supportive wider family helped her find her own courage and claim her options to move on.

Mobility is a reality, and it makes us hungry for steady, healthy relationships. How many people appear in all of the chapters of your life? Precious is the experience of knowing and being known continuously through all the stages of life. Each chapter of life has its tasks and rhythms that call forth certain types of commitments, some for a very short duration. Our friendships and working relationships for that period may be extremely enjoyable and energizing. And then circumstances dictate that one of us moves on. There remains a hunger for someone you can count on no matter where you live and no matter how long since you have actually been together.

## Commitments That Nurture and Sustain

What fosters the healthy commitments for which we all long? Some committed relationships seem merely to evolve. Others are a terrible struggle. Some people seem more able than others to make and keep commitments. What gives them the staying power?

How can we nurture healthy committed relationships of mutual promise keeping?

First, we need to know that keeping promises in a world of infidelity is not foolish. Hard maybe, but not foolish. We may feel foolish when we extend ourselves responsibly only to be negated, rejected, or betrayed. But our identity and worth need not be dependent on others keeping their promises.

Second, God is a God of unconditional love; human beings seem to put conditions on everything. We will keep a promise to a friend as long as that person meets our explicit (or implicit) expectations. When a neighbor doesn't keep a promise to clear underbrush, we threaten to sue. Why not let go of our tight grip on our handful of conditions and try freely sharing ourselves? We might be surprised at what this produces.

Third, in a healthy relationship we can call forth the gifts of the other person, realizing that both of us are called to love, serve, and give of ourselves. We may never reach a totally balanced interdependence, but we can explore the varieties of resources each of us brings to the relationship. One of us may be more experienced. The other brings new insight. One is older or younger; the other stronger. One brings gifts of laughter; the other of organization. One possesses far-reaching knowledge; the other focused perception. Each of us may have what can help the other grow, and together we can offer something to the world beyond our relationship.

We are finite beings with limitations. But we are capable of making and sustaining commitments. We may need to sort out which commitments no longer need to be maintained and jointly decide to conclude them. We will need to listen carefully, and we will want to be fair. Even so, there will be misunderstandings and even some pain. Yet we can dare to make commitments and, seeking support outside ourselves, we can give attention to the commitments we have made and help them nurture the other and ourselves as well.

In personal and professional partnerships, we can make commitments to each other that in themselves then sustain us in the times when faithfulness seems hard. The commitment, then, itself provides the freedom simply to be and live, knowing the relationship is in place; we can use the energy, not in finding a new partner, but in being one.

## Promises for Our Promise Making

God's promises permeate, undergird, and transform our promise making and promise keeping:

1. God has created us for healthy interdependence. All people face loneliness and hunger for community. We can reach out to form a new relationship, sharing both our strengths and needs.

2. God who is trustworthy has kept and will keep the promise to

love us unconditionally. We can trust God's love, especially in times
when no one seems to care about us. We can also dare to love steadfast-
ly, even in a commitment that seems to be failing.

3. Christ knows betrayal. We may still feel the sting of the times
when we were betrayed. Forgiveness means letting go of the grudge and
the plans for retaliation. We can know, also, that we do not need to continue to be crucified. Christ's cross was sufficient.

4. God's forgiveness in Christ gives us freedom to acknowledge
broken promises. We can let the defenses fall and accept instead Christ's
forgiveness. We can then explore the freedom to reestablish a relationship, to renew a commitment, to go some new directions.

5. God gives us identity in baptism. We can claim God's name and
know who and whose we are. We can be free to give of ourselves in
carrying out a commitment, knowing our identity is secure.

6. God's Spirit fills us with new life. In discerning the gifts we
have, we can accept a calling to a new commitment. That may mean
closing a commitment that is unhealthy or no longer uses our gifts.

7. God places us in Christian community giving us to each other as
God's commitment. We can receive people—ordinary though they are—
as brothers and sisters in Christ, refusing to place guilt-producing claims
on each other. Seeing each other as God's gift, we can live out our commitments.

## Discussion

1.   With what people do you have a life-long commitment?
2.   How do you sustain and nourish those commitments?
3.   What relation do your long-term commitments have to your situ-
     ational day-to-day commitments?

## CHAPTER 2

# Doubting Our Worth

While on any given day our packed schedules prevent much reflection, just beneath the surface doubting questions of worth prick: *What am I really doing running myself ragged like this? Where am I going? What in the world does this all mean?* Tired, or criticized, we may want to throw in the towel or throw the towel at someone. But we keep running, perhaps to avoid those basic questions and nagging doubts.

*Is it worth it?* people ask, concerning their investments of time, love, money, membership, or friendship. We wonder, *Which of these is worth the most to me?* We doubt, *Are any of these worth investing myself in?* Soon we entertain haunting doubts about our own worth: *Am I doing enough? Do they really want to spend time with me, or is it merely obligation? What am I worth to them?* We doubt and are doubted.

We keep these questions submerged because to surface them, we assume, would diminish our worth in others' eyes. Because those "others" do the same, we rarely see one another's inner struggles. *She always seems to have it all together; why can't I be like that?* Or, *If I made the money he makes, I'd be sure of myself.* Or, romanticizing the past, *Wouldn't it be nice to have lived when people could trust one another, when society had values?* The questions of worth and doubt trouble each of us to some degree whatever our economic class, age, culture, gender, or period in history. Racism, sexism, and classism intensify the struggle, keeping oppressed and oppressor in bondage to predetermined judgments of worth. These struggles are the stuff of human drama, so that's where we begin.

Doubting our worth is both human and haunting. We seem to need to know we have intrinsic worth, particularly when at the end of the day we feel no validation, either because our doubts kept us from hearing someone's affirmation, or because it simply wasn't there. Demands wear us down until it's hard to sort out the source of the struggle. We wonder if we'll ever feel certain of ourselves. To avoid the questions merely prolongs the struggle.

**Reflection**

Take time to do that for which there is no time:

1.  Reflect on several of the many demands of your life and about some of the doubts you may have about them.
2.  Find a quiet place to think about, or perhaps write down, some of your responses to this question:  Is this (task, relationship, etc.) worth it?
3.  What inner doubts about self-worth might you harbor, just beneath the surface?

## The Ambiguities of Living in the World

We live in a world that engenders doubtfulness. It's no wonder we doubt our worth. Because we live in many diverse but intersecting worlds—of work, home, and leisure—and because those worlds have competing value and meaning systems, different ways of measuring worth, we are torn by multiple loyalties. Those who are invested in our worth often make ambiguous demands on us. For example, the firm demands allegiance to an unwritten company policy that high sales outweigh personal values. The family says your time at home is worth a great deal to them. On the other hand, the family expects yearly raises, and the division manager wonders if sales come before loyalty to long-time employees.

By definition, *ambiguity* admits to more than one meaning, which is not bad, but competing or even contradictory meanings raise anxiety. When we are uncertain, we may feel not only doubt, but also fear. How can we give allegiance to all those forces that clamor to be worth the most in our lives?  To struggle with what is worth most in life and to doubt one's worth are ultimately spiritual struggles. We need something or someone to assure us of our worth, and we need a center in the midst of multiple claims of ultimate worth. Those multiple worlds in which we live collectively make for an ambiguous environment that is confusing. Sometimes it is supportive; more often it is hostile or indifferent to our faith and sense of what is worthwhile.

## Meet Karen

Karen introduces herself as a "professional person," although she currently is not "employed" in the sense of receiving a salary for one particular job. She holds a master's degree and in the past has worked in positions that were generally supportive of or related to her concerns for soci-ety (i.e., education, the environment).

Karen went through a period of deep depression when she was let go from her last job. Currently she keeps very active in volunteer organizations and associations such as American Association of University Women. She serves on the board of the YWCA battered women's shelter and is a rape crisis counselor. She keeps up on current issues and regularly shares her insights and opinions at her adult Bible study group.

This past year Karen has been almost overwhelmed in the roles of daughter and daughter-in-law; because both her mother and mother-in-law have been ill, she has spent a great deal of time in each of their homes during their recoveries. Now, she says, "It's time to be 'me'!" She tries to be supportive of her husband, who puts in a lot of overtime at work. She keeps in contact with her adult son, who lives away, and she tries to connect with her thirteen-year-old son who is very bright, but uncommunicative.

In many ways Karen is very intentional about how she understands the connections between her faith and daily life. She reaches out to others in places and ways that most people in her congregation would not recognize as being related to Christian ministry or concerns of the church. Karen struggles with her identity and worth apart from what she "does."

1.  What are the issues of "worth" in Karen's story?

2.  How do role and identity shape her struggle?

3.  Do you know a "Karen"?  What elements of her story are similar to your own or that of someone you care about?

Not only do we face ambiguity about questions of worth from the world, but those competing messages are also inside of us. We have been nurtured in a multifaceted culture that has formed and shaped competing value systems—in our daily worlds and inside our homes, hearts, and heads. Each of us is acting on a variety of belief systems at any given time. And demands of employment, acquaintances, creditors, and community compound our confusion—about priorities and beliefs and values. Even our belief in God.

Our spiritual doubts are of many kinds, perhaps about the existence of God. But few people claim to be outright atheists. More likely the spiritual doubts concern the confusing combination of images of what produces the good life: the lottery, angels, good luck, good deeds, prayer, health foods. What do we believe?  In whom do we believe?  Even the reports about what food is healthy change from week to week. We seek clarity but continue in the confusion, accepting as normal our being caught in the web. And God seems to be caught in our little web, too.

Our lives work well on the days when the sun is shining, the car starts, there are no traffic jams, the baby-sitter is not sick, and the lines at the drive-in teller and dry cleaner are not too long. But when all is not going well (or maybe even when it is), the doubt creeps in: *I always pick the longest line at the check-out counter.* (Doubt: *Why don't I seem to be able to get it right?*) *Others at my workplace know how to be noticed and rewarded.* (Doubt: *Am I not as productive, worthwhile, as they, or have I simply learned from my Christian upbringing not to flaunt my success?*) *I seem to be important to my family and associates.* (Doubt: *Is that simply as long as I give them what they need?  Do they value me for me?*)

Struggling with competing meaning systems may seem normal, but it is still disconcerting. Pressured by demands of work, family, and self, where in the world are we, and what in the world does this mean?

**Discuss with Someone You Trust**

1.   What competing voices about what is worthwhile might you hear on any given day?
2.   What inner mixed messages guide your decision making throughout the day?
3.   What doubts do you have about those demands and those values?
4.   How is this issue a spiritual struggle for you?

## "Worthship" in our World

If doubt concerning our own worth and what's worth our time and attention are spiritual struggles, the confused and confusing worlds in which we live don't help us very much in the task of centering our lives. Hundreds of images, ideas, and demands bombard us daily: *Notice me! This alone is worthy of your attention!* We need to doubt their competing claims. More often we doubt ourselves—and our own worth in their eyes. We don't measure up to the advertising image. We haven't attained financial success. We need to ask if such advertising claims are true. What's more, we need to ask if what they promise is worth our pursuit.

That to which we commit ourselves, pledge our loyalty, give our resources—that around which we plan our lives—needs to be worthy of such devotion. Ann has worked hard to put herself through graduate school, but the corporation where she finally landed a job demands ("if she's planning on a career here") not only all her time, but also ten years of moving to any location they choose for her. Is the sacrifice worth the career? Ann must decide. Brian, who grew up in an unstable family, is devoted to his own children. But now that they've reached teenage years, he realizes his love may be misguiding in not providing the disciplined boundaries they need, and misguided because his children cannot replace the love he lost as a child.

We may have more important goals than winning the lottery or becoming the most popular, but even the most noble goals in the world are not worth our worship, for goals are not worthy gods; ultimately they are not trustworthy.

"But," we say, "I don't worship my job or my husband or my retirement investments." Of course not—at least not consciously and by name. Most of us say we believe in God and pray and even frequently experience God's care and guidance in the midst of difficulties. But for the most part, with God tucked safely inside Sunday church walls, people feel they have to go it on their own during the week. God's house of worship is a place to relax and refuel, even a place of refuge at times. The doubts of self-worth and the rat-race of work seem totally separate from the spiritual.

It may be, however, that we can find the source of the struggle by asking the spiritual questions of those things that make their claims of worth all week. We can walk around our worlds, literally and figuratively. Who and what fill my day? In what causes do I invest my time and energy? What worries me and causes sleepless nights? Who intimidates me? Whom or what do I love? Whom or what would I miss most? In whom, in what, do I trust? That which we fear, love, and trust above all, some would say, are our gods. Are they worthy gods?

Beneath the hundreds of decisions people make each day are goals, undergirded by values, grounded in beliefs about ultimate worth: our gods. If I am a real estate agent, my task will be to sell houses. I also need to develop a clientele that trusts my agency enough to list its property for sale. The type of property listed and the neighborhoods where signs go up advertise the status of the agency. Underlying these goals will be value judgments concerning economics, class, race, and community, which may or may not be shared by all who work for this agency. Does every person have the right to own a home? What is more important—private economic security or the needs of the community? Does diversity of people in the neighborhood enhance the quality of life? What do we believe is of ultimate worth?

## Beliefs Shape Actions and Actions Shape Beliefs

While many of our beliefs may never be articulated, all of us hold basic beliefs. Not only do beliefs shape actions, but actions shape the ongoing formulation of beliefs. The repeated exercise of making decisions reinforces even unarticulated belief systems. The daily routine in our complex worlds may seem to have little to do with spirituality, or with "gods," but goals, values, beliefs, and what we hold of ultimate worth are all about trust and faith and spirituality.

The claims on our life as to what is worthwhile bombard us, and to survive impending chaos, we create our own world of worth. And for a while that all works. On most Mondays—and maybe even on some Fridays—our doubts are in check, our self-worth intact, our values are in place, and our lives are in balance. But then the questions of worth resurface. Our doubts do not so much condemn us as call for a time for self-reflection. It's hard to do such reflection alone. Later in the book we will consider ways we can help one another in this regard. But, for now, we need to start where we are and come to grips with the nature of worth and the dilemmas of doubt.

It's in times of crisis that the doubts come out of hiding. It's when values are in shambles that people ask questions. But if God is more than a God of last resorts, it might be worth it not to wait for a crisis but to take a look at that which we do hold in ultimate worth all day and all night long.

**Reflection**

1.   Take one aspect of your daily work and trace backwards:  What are my actions . . . my decisions . . . my goals . . . my values . . . my beliefs . . . my gods?
2.   How is "worthship" related to worship?

## Claiming Our Worth and Worshipping What Really Claims Us

This society is not so much devoid of God as it is doubtful of the worth of the gods we continually set before us. Because of the highly competitive world, the multiple goals people must pursue compel them to place value and trust in many varied people, principles, and pursuits in an ever-changing culture. Little lasts and that which does is doubted. Again, we generally do not doubt that we have gods; we doubt because the gods that claim us are not of ultimate worth.

In the midst of a competitive society, one gains advantage by keeping the other on edge, in doubt of her ability, his worth, and, if possible, her very core being. We are created for interdependence, for seeing and enhancing the worth of each other and for mutual, accountable cooperation. But it is easier, and quicker, to tear down another's worth.

The revolving door of political leaders testifies to the need for someone to trust and to our suspicion that they are not worthy of trust. They are not worthy of ultimate trust, of course. Trusting completely in oneself is foolish, and trusting completely in another is dangerous. Feeling powerless, people retreat further into cynicism, daring to step into the world of public debate only through the anonymity of call-in talk shows. In the absence of a deep sense of worth, our fear of one another intensifies, and we seek radical forms of self-protection. Soon we become armed camps.

To be free to make healthy commitments to God, to others, and to ourselves, we need to address the claims that have claimed us. Only when people know they are worthwhile to God, and to one another, can they sort out worthy goals. We cannot do this on our own. We need to *hear* we are worth something to others. We need each other to help us understand that which claims us. And we need to hear a Word of unconditional love from God to release us from our doubts and from pursuing unworthy gods. In so doing we can claim the worth God has invested in us and worship the one God who claims us all as beloved.

We all doubt. Self-doubt reveals doubts about God and doubts about God deepen our doubts about ourselves. Recognizing this dilemma is a good beginning so that rather than trying to compensate for doubts through cynicism, mutual suspicion, and dangerous reaction, we can seek and depend on a God who is worthy of ultimate trust and who has no doubt about the value of every human being.

**Action**

1. Remember the doubts you wrote down earlier? In a small group or with a trusted friend dare to say them aloud.
2. Having spoken, listen carefully for a word of worthwhileness from another.
3. Hear out someone else's doubts. Give careful attention and respond to each other with a word of hope, not simply, "That's okay; we all have doubts," but a genuine good word of grace, that God values and loves and is willing to forgive and heal and empower each of us to live in the world.

CHAPTER 3

# *Feeling the Pressure*

Longing for commitment and doubting our worth are basic human struggles, often so deep that struggles may be imperceptible in daily life. The stress-producing pressures of daily life may be all too perceptible.

With all of our labor-saving devices, we seem to be busier, more tired, and under greater stress than ever before. Why do we do this to ourselves? Or do we? The pressures are mostly external, aren't they? And how is stress related to our faith?

Do you know Alexander? He's the seven- or eight-year-old nonhero of the great children's book *Alexander and the Terrible, Horrible, No Good, Very Bad Day*. Absolutely nothing goes right from the time he gets up, and every minute of his day is filled with trouble and disappointment:

> I went to sleep with gum in my mouth and now there's gum in my hair and when I got out of bed this morning I tripped on the skateboard and by mistake I dropped my sweater in the sink while the water was running.

He meets all kinds of difficulties at school, the dentist's office, and the shoe store. His troubles continue right up to the end of the day when he sums it all up: "It has been a terrible, horrible, no good, very bad day."[1]

Talk about stress! Talk about being overwhelmed! Alexander has had it all!

## Signs and Symptoms of Stress

Adults as well as children relate to Alexander. We know stress and have experienced its signs: loss of breath, sweaty palms, rapid heartbeat. Under stress we feel pressure and tension; our adrenaline flows. Our behavior changes; we eat and walk rapidly; we become impatient with others and even ourselves; we feel guilty about relaxing. We are torn between demands at our work and our personal relationships. Both time and energy are in short supply. We don't know how to keep on keeping on.

Stress can be described as our physical response to anything that excites, upsets, or threatens. It may be a feeling of being squeezed by too many demands from too many directions. Stress can come from increased demands, or even decreased demands, such as the first weeks of retirement. We encounter stress in crisis. Who can forget that awful moment when someone entered the room with life-changing tragic news of a family member injured in an accident?

When we experience the extreme stress of crisis or even continuous daily stress, sleep can come slowly, if at all. Norma's mother used to talk about being tired at night, but she'd say it was a "good tired," meaning a satisfied fatigue from a full day's work; such a fatigue readied her for restful sleep. That's different from the fitful, binding stress that is unhealthy; when we seem caught in binds, unable to extricate ourselves, neither work nor a break from work is satisfying.

### Reflection

1.  Recall a day last week that, if not quite like Alexander's, had its "terrible, horrible, not good, very bad" moments.
2.  What started it? What continued it? What happened inside of you in the midst of the stress?
3.  What are some physical signs that you may be regularly under undue stress?

## Dealing with Stress

One commentator has said that most people successfully handle 98 percent of the potentially stressful activities that confront them every day. That leaves only 2 percent to give us serious trouble. But it's usually that 2 percent that causes 98 percent of our stress. We cannot and should not ignore stress. Stress is a part of everyone's life; Christians are not immune. We all have to deal with it.

We begin to deal with stress by being aware of how it works. Stress is normally thought of as a negative influence, but to some extent it is helpful. Stress is not simply pressure from the outside; it is also the physical reaction within the body that prepares us to meet life's disturbing situations. Some stress is destructive because it gnaws and saps energy. But some stress can be good; it sharpens concentration and stimulates creativity.

Stress can be used constructively when we neither over- nor underreact. Under stress, as one writer has said, we are apt to spend ten dollars' worth of adrenaline on a ten-cent problem. To overreact is to deplete our energy resources. But to underreact may also cause difficulty.

To ignore a festering problem at work—to allow a relationship to disintegrate—is to spend ten dollars' worth of adrenaline on a hundred-dollar problem. Only later do we realize how crucial a problem the festering symptom was calling to our attention—how important the relationship was.

Stress is the body's alarm system. When we must act, stress prepares us to do so. Stress becomes harmful when the defense system works overtime or never shuts down. Then excessive stress becomes "distress" that shows itself in anxiety, tension, and depression.

---

### Meet Jim

Jim, a manager with a public gas and electric utility, supervises a group of engineers and technical and support staff. He is married, has two grown sons, and is very involved in his congregation. Although he finds it difficult to connect his religious faith with his workplace, he tries to model a Christian life in his role as a manager and tries to be supportive of people facing crises and transitions.

Lately Jim's employer has been downsizing; many people have been laid off. This has been a very stressful time for Jim, who has to balance the needs of many constituencies. As a public utility, the corporation is accountable to rate-paying customers, stockholders, employees, communities, regulators, suppliers, and the general public. Sometimes one of these constituencies becomes greedy and causes stress for the others.

As a manager Jim is under pressure to make responsible decisions affecting many people, only some of whom he knows personally. His job involves a constant balancing act of loyalty to staff and employers and the public.

Jim feels that very few people in the congregation know what he faces each day. Although he sings in the choir and is church council president, his church activities don't connect him with the issues he faces in daily life. Although he knows people in church care about him and he does feel spiritual renewal in general, because parishioners don't talk about each other's lives on the job, his Sunday worship experience and daily faith life and ministry remain disconnected.

When Jim was challenged to imagine what church might mean for him if we began with the assumption that all Christians are already in ministry, that people are encouraged to bring their struggles and joys to the congregation's worship, and that his ministry in daily life *is* church work, he said he had never thought about that. He became excited as he began to think about church not simply representing one more thing to do, one more decision to make, or one more obligation to keep. As he thought aloud, Jim mentioned a Bible study group where he felt he could talk through his struggles, stresses, and concerns and that could help him live out his faith.

1.  How do the demands of conflicting constituents impact Jim—and us?

2.  How might a faith community be open to people talking about their struggles and stresses?

It is essential that we bring our daily stress and our faith together. If we see all the tensions as negative and if our faith stays isolated in worship and prayer, we only deny and bury our anxiety. When stress is happening, God is still present and is at work in our lives. If we think our faith is healthy only when life seems calm and peaceful, we are missing the point. In the midst of the frustrating relationship with a co-worker, the tense distance with a child or a parent, the ongoing conflict about what is needed to keep the congregation financially solvent, the Christ who knew struggle, even agony, is struggling with us. In all such stressful situations, although it is sometimes difficult to see at the time, the Holy Spirit is opening us to new direction and growth.

## Stress and the Church

"I'm too tired to take on one more thing." When our lives are already full of stress, the last thing we want is to take on an extra assignment at church. Even one more responsibility feels more like a demand than a request. Conflicts and disagreements within the congregation can aggravate tension. Personality differences among church leaders add to the stress level. Simply maintaining the congregation seems to take all our time and energy and money.

Who needs all these problems? Television, magazines, newspapers—all portray the weekend as just that, a time to end the week, get away, be with family, be entertained. If we don't find Sunday worship energizing, what's the problem? Something wrong with the church? Something wrong with us?

When we are too stressed out to really "get into church," it may be because we are looking merely for sanctuary, something removed from, remote from everyday life. The institution called church, a gathering of human beings, also has a "daily life" with all the potential for misunderstanding and struggle. A building, even a congregation, cannot be holy— a sanctuary—in and of itself. But it can be, it *is*, a place where God is in the midst of the community, loving, forgiving, and shaping the people for renewal.

The faith community may be exhausted because it feeds only itself. When bored, the people begin to bicker; when stressed out, they blame one another. The congregation may gain energy by moving beyond mere maintenance to exercising ministry outside its own walls. The church will never be free of stress, but there we learn how God can transform stressed-out people as they share themselves with others.

**Reflection**

Recall faith communities of which you have been or are a part.

1. When did you feel more stressed out, when you left or when you arrived?
2. Recall some worship experiences or faith-education groups in which you were able to really talk about the pressures of daily life and where participants energized one another with the Spirit. What happened in the groups that made a difference?
3. How could you help create such opportunities in the future for yourself and/or others?

## Clergy Feel Pressures Too

We're all part of the *laos,* the whole people of God. We place unnecessary barriers between us when we buy into the game of who has it harder, clergy or laity. We get nowhere when we play games of one-upmanship about who is more stressed out (perhaps that would be one-downmanship; "you think you have it rough . . . "). The truth is, we all feel stress. More often than not, we intensify one another's stress when we refuse to understand the pressures others face.

Even though churches are committed to mission, the full, long journey of mission in the world is rarely fully explored and gives way to pressure to measure mission in terms of numbers of Sunday worshippers and the size of the budget. Simply put: Clergy feel overburdened, pressured by judicatory leaders, other clergy, and parishioners themselves to make successful churches. They may want to walk with laity into their worlds, but where's the time?

While many clergy are fully committed to the concept of ministry in daily life and respect deeply the parishioners among whom they serve, the congregational and broader church structures often do not reward pastors for being interested in and upholding parishioners' work in the world. And the stress increases.

## We Are Called to Care

Three pivotal affirmations can help us deal with stress: God cares for us, really cares for us; God wants us to take care of ourselves; and we are called to care for one another. Weaving these three beliefs deep into our daily lives will not eliminate stress, but it can help us deal with the inevitable stress within and around us, including the tensions within our faith community.

A real sense of inner peace comes only from God. All of us seek spiritual meaning and depth and want to find an inner source of strength. We are empowered by the Spirit and that Spirit connects us in Christ in ways that both refresh and energize us to serve; spirituality means being connected to God and to others in ways that give life.

## Disciplines for the Journey

To function well, the body and spirit and mind all need certain rhythms such as eating and resting properly, regular exercise, and laughter—surely one of God's greatest gifts. Christians who constantly worry are not really effective witnesses for Christ. When stress builds up, something as simple as taking a few moments to breathe deeply and stretch may be the first step to deal with the tense situation. Each of these activities nurtures the self. Sometimes we need to recognize that instead of acting in a hurry, we need to wait in faith. Our bodies and spirits and minds are gifts from God to be cared for with respect; we need not self-destruct in anxiety and tension.

There's a direct relationship between the outer journey (often treacherous) toward ministry in daily life and the inner journey of spirituality grounded in Scripture and prayer.

> Since you have accepted Christ Jesus as Lord, live in union with him. Keep your roots deep in him, build your lives on him, and become stronger in your faith, as you were taught. And be filled with thanksgiving (Col. 2:6-7 TEV).

To become more Christ-conscious—to live more deeply in Christ—means to be nourished by the "rivers of living water" (John 7:38). Without being rooted in Christ, we are apt to die of lack of spiritual nourishment.

To be in union with Christ is to be both spiritually alive and worldly active. We need not divide the contemplative and the worldly, God-talk and human-talk. Inner transformation is the work of God; it is our privilege to develop and grow through a definite plan of prayer and regular meditation with the Bible. Discipline implies a deliberate endeavor, a sticking-to-it in spite of moods, even during heavy stress. We need prayer exactly when we have closed ourselves to God and others; that is when we most need God—and love. I (Nelvin) think of my daughter—she instinctively knew that when I came home tense and angry, that was when I most needed a hug.

Just when we feel too stressed from our activity in the world to pray or to reach out to someone or even to receive another person's initiative, the very discipline of connecting provides a way for God to relieve the pressure.

## Meet Rita

Rita decided to take some much needed rest and relaxation. Because she did not have to work—teach school—last week, she made arrangements to visit some friends in Phoenix. This get-away was precipitated by the placement of her mother in an Alzheimer's care facility. For two years Rita had cared for her mother at home, employing various support services. There had been no family support; her father is deceased and her only sibling is a missionary in Africa.

After her mother's move, Rita felt drained, both physically and emotionally. "I didn't realize how much this was taking out of me," she said. In addition to all this, she had taken on a student teacher in her classroom who was not working out very well. She was ready for a vacation. As a woman of prayer, she was so accustomed to giving herself to others, she didn't realize she needed not only a vacation, but also ministry.

Shortly after Rita arrived in Phoenix, she learned that her mother had fallen and broken her hip. Friends from church took over the visitation schedule and surgery vigil to allow Rita to stay in Phoenix. Her friends realized that if she did not have time to relax, she would not have the energy to meet the challenges she would face upon returning home.

Now Rita is home, making the two-hour trip to see her mother at least once a week. She has the same hectic schedule, teaching all day, meetings or other church activities at night, and also worrying about her mother's deteriorating health. She prays for personal strength and now she also knows that when things become overwhelming, she needs to take a break, and she knows she's not alone. The people who gather for worship weekly are also eager to minister to each other to build up the body of Christ.

Rita has asked for the prayers of others. She knows she will continue to need friends to sustain and energize her. A feeling of the Spirit flowing through her faith community,

connecting them and her mother across the miles, is important to her. She knows that spiritual and emotional support
are as important as physical support.

1. When have you been so drained that you did not even
   know it?

2. In what tangible ways have you experienced support
   from a faith community in the midst of the struggle?

3. Are there concrete ways now you can ask for and offer
   someone physical, emotional, spiritual support?

## God Cares through Care for One Another

Sometimes the very act of reaching out for help is stressful. When we
need to be ministered to, we may not have the energy or the courage to
reach out to gather strength from the very people who may stand ready to
help. We do not listen to those we trust. Frequently we do not even admit
our struggles.

Amid stress, the question comes: How do we keep on keeping on?
Even our denial of need is forgiven through the Cross. When we by
God's grace recognize the need to be renewed, the Spirit can begin to
refresh and reenergize us. The people of God see the need to reach out,
to be sustained by the strength of others.[2] We do not walk alone in the
body of Christ. We are revitalized to strengthen others, whether members
of the body of Christ or not. Therefore the empty tomb can regenerate
hope.

The paradox is that if we reach out to serve others, the stress within
is lessened. Instead of being overly concerned with self, we see the needs
and hopes of others. Instead of looking only at the immediate, we see the
perspective of our communal past and God's promised future.

## CHAPTER 4

# Struggling with Power

"We seem to have a power struggle here." Is that a way of saying, "I don't like the way you are doing your job," or perhaps, "I sense conflict and don't know what to do about it"? It simply may be a social comment on the ways we regularly relate to each other. Power and authority, responsibility, and relationship are the stuff of everyday life and the source of many a pain in the neck or ache in the stomach. One could talk about all of life as a struggle over power, who has it and who doesn't.

Of all the doubts and struggles we face, the issue of power is one of the most difficult. Power is fundamentally energy, the ability to make something happen. We all have power. Even the powerless, the oppressed, the disenfranchised possess potential for revolt. Power *per se* is not evil. We can use it for healthy or deathly goals.

We can empower people or abuse them with our power. We recognize empowerment when we hear, "Your taking time to walk me through the task made all the difference," or, "Thanks, those resources were exactly what I needed." We experience abusive power when we feel used, silenced, shamed, saying to ourselves, *He's always angry, there must be something wrong with me.* We abuse power when we insist people over whom we have authority respond to our every whim, when we intimidate or ignore. We can slowly kill someone's spirit by words or actions that say, *You really aren't worth much; you aren't needed here.*

We cannot avoid power by pretending that our lives are unaffected by its use. We have power. We need power. We use power. We need to share power. Even if we contend Christians don't engage in power struggles, the truth is all people use and abuse power. To believe Christians should not concern themselves with power is not only naive, but dangerous, not just because someone might take advantage of us, but dangerous insofar as we are likely to abuse others without even recognizing it. We all have power and need power to live and to be in ministry in our daily lives.

**Reflection**

1. How do you exercise power? How does that vary depending upon your role and relationship?
2. When do you feel powerless? Where do you believe you have more power than appropriate?
3. How do you use power to effect change?

## Sharing Unlimited Power

We can learn to share power. If we operate thinking power is limited, we will hoard it. In that scheme, your having more power means I have less. A pastor is threatened when a lay leader excels. A committee is tempted to ignore a newcomer's gifts. We have learned well how to count and compete. But if we believe that power is unlimited and can multiply, we act differently. I need not fear your having power if neither of us abuses it or seeks to dominate. In fact, when you are energized, generating ideas, accomplishing goals, your power can increase my own. I am more energized, more able to do my work. Your power doesn't lessen mine, and my power in turn enhances yours. We encourage, excite, and empower one another. Using our energy together we actually accomplish more than each of us working alone. Together we multiply gifts and have the potential of empowering others.

"Idealistic!" you say. Indeed! Listening to the daily news or to cafeteria conversations, we usually hear about power being used over and against another person. Who won the match? How do we get ahead of the competition? Who made points in the debate? Did we regain our turf? Even noncontroversial issues are reported as one party gaining advantage. Fights entertain—at least the spectators. But if life is more than a spectator sport, we need to move beyond an up/down perspective toward healthy interdependence. It's not merely idealistic, but a matter of life and death in every relationship, from the family to the global community.

Shared power seems to be the antithesis of competitive power. What is the role of healthy competition? Some people say they work best in competitive situations. Competition can motivate. It also can kill. Competition is healthy when we know power is not limited, when we recognize that our using muscles and developing gifts encourages others. As companions jogging alongside one another, we set a pace that is mutually challenging. But pushing and driving until one or the other drops out or drops dead leaves one a winner, but alone. Being on top may mean I'm a leader, but there may be no one else around to lead. It's lonely at the top. To have all the power may ultimately mean to have no power.

**Reflection**

Recall a situation in which cooperative power energized a group. Mentally re-create some of the dynamics.

1. How did people generate ideas?
2. How did they share power? Divide responsibilities? Encourage growth?
3. What were the dynamics? What was the outcome?

## Exercising Appropriate Authority

Power and authority are related but not synonymous. Authority, by some definitions, is legitimate power. One can have authority and little power. One can use power without authorization.

We perceive many of our daily struggles to be about roles and authority relationships. We say, "My boss is on my back all day," or, "My subordinates won't get to work on time and don't use their time at work effectively."

From early childhood we become so used to living in the shadows of authority relationships that as adults we unconsciously check to see if there's a highway patrol person around the next bend. At lunch with a friend we joke that we can't stay for dessert because the boss will be watching the time clock. We blame some unknown future tax auditor for making us check and recheck our work. One could argue that fear of what authorities might do to us keeps the world running in relative order. But when we are motivated only through fear of someone else's authority, we abdicate our own authority, our own responsibility for our lives.

To live in the fear of someone else's authority is to live reactively. It keeps us forever off the hook. We remain children to whomever we make a parent. We diminish ourselves and never grow to maturity. And we live in a dulled state, literally petrified, unable to use the energy, the power, we do have to enliven the world around us.

If we believe we have been created for interdependence in a variety of roles in a myriad of relationships, our lives are complex, but we do have some authority and some power with which to make wise decisions. If we believe some people were created to rule and others to be subordinate, we will never reach creative interdependence. We are variously gifted, and everyone's gifts are necessary for a healthy, productive society. We can either use our power to destroy one another, living forever in fear, or, together, we can build a world in which all can live together.

In our ordinary lives, of course, there are things to fear. Not all people act with others' best interests in mind. How can we trust those with power to exercise it well? Even those who exercise power legitimated by authority may abuse their office. Those who use power to commit random acts of violence are a danger in the community. There are children who bully around the block and nations that bully around the globe.

People who feel powerless in one situation may exercise abusive power in a situation where they can get away with it. In pecking order, when we have been kicked, we tend to kick the person occupying the next lower position than ourselves. We eventually go home and kick the dog, or the spouse whom we treat like a dog, or the children, or our elderly parents. Or we may act out our frustrations in a church committee.

Sometimes we even wonder if we can trust ourselves faithfully to exercise the authority we do have. History and the daily news have too many stories of misuse of both power and authority to allow us to rest easily. It's easy to become very discouraged. The abuse of power can get us down.

# Meet Jan

Jan is a fifty-four-year-old audiologist. Even though she's very competent and has a good business, she says, "I hate to go to work." She feels trapped but is unable to visualize any other options. She works with four physicians, and, although she has a Ph.D., she is not considered a peer. She's at an age when she needs to think about security, but she would like to change to another practice. She recently had open-heart surgery and believes she can't risk a job change because with the preexisting condition she will be unable to get health insurance.

The most satisfying part of her job is when she is able to help patients put words to their experience of hearing loss. The hardest part is telling parents their child is hard of hearing. She does not want to give false hope, and she empathizes with their terrible disappointment when they finally admit what they really knew but had denied. Jan could quickly use her power of expertise to inform (and perhaps overwhelm) them, but rather she schedules another appointment for a later time when they will be able to absorb the information and perhaps be empowered to seek answers.

Jan struggles with the legal implications of medicine today. She says, "You always have to be aware you could be sued." And yet Jan is adamant that no one controls her work or should question her professional decisions. She holds a strong conviction she will not prescribe hearing aids if they are not needed. That is a line she will not cross. Jan sometimes feels powerless in the lives of people she would like to help and can't.

But the greatest source of stress is the power politics in the office. Jan wants to exercise her authority helpfully and meaningfully. As a Christian she has thought about servanthood in terms of emptying oneself, but she hasn't thought about what this has to do with power. She participates in weekend retreats through a program at church. This has been a place she feels she can talk about her feelings and pain and help others who are going through difficult times.

1.  What are the issues of power in Jan's story?

2.  What authority does Jan have and not have?

3.  Understanding the limits to one's authority, how can Jan (or you) use power appropriately?

## Resurrection, Reconciliation, and Relinquishment

*Resurrection* and *reconciliation* are religious words and more than mere words; they are strong belief concepts applied to real life and death situations. Whereas power struggles that produce a revolution usually result in power holders being conquered and killed, resurrection reminds us that Christ is alive and intends to share that life with all. No one is killed. The power that is defeated is death itself.

When the people of the Philippines in 1986 called for people power and won the elections and then had to upset those in power to place the winning woman in power, broadcasters searched for words to describe what they were seeing. It was not so much a revolution as a resurrection. People were not killing, but turning things around with a power for life.

Reconciliation is power to befriend and forgive and to live in peace in new relationships. Reconciliation is as new and radical as the Gospel itself. The very ones who once struggled now seek new ways to live at peace.

Namibia, after winning independence from South African rule in 1990, chose not to retaliate after years of oppressive apartheid. The key postindependence word in Namibia is *reconciliation*! The expected retaliation is replaced with new potential for understanding and new, right relationships. Resurrection and reconciliation don't happen all the time, but they happen enough to help us know such good news is possible.

Barbara Jordan, who during her lieftime served as a congresswoman from Texas, constitutional scholar, and professor, said that you cannot give power to others, but you can allow them to claim their own. Sr. Marie Augusta Neal teaches a theology of relinquishment.[1] We may feel frustrated that people hesitate to claim their own power. But here we suggest strategies to empower by relinquishing control, by freeing up the situation so others can claim and use their own power. This is risky, of course, but no more risky than continuing to control.

## Strategies to Empower by Relinquishing Control

1. When I try to give others power, I may appear to be patronizing, but when I relinquish some of my power and wait patiently with them as they find their own voices, choose their own directions, and achieve their own goals, I can rejoice with their accomplishment; what's more, I may learn something new from them.

2. Knowing the Spirit's power is unlimited, I can genuinely encourage others to claim their gifts, become skilled, use their abilities, and exercise power over their own lives, knowing I will not lose any personal power but might gain colleagues.

3. No one was created for absolute submission to anyone else's power. Neither were we created for domination over people. Christ alone is *dominus,* "Lord." When I am beginning to have more power in a relationship than is healthy, I can relinquish the emerging tendency to "lord" it over by refusing to play that role.

4. Many power struggles can be alleviated by clarifying roles and relationships. When I find my identity in my role, I fear losing that position. But when my identity is rooted in my baptism in Christ, I know I cannot lose that identity. Then I can play the appropriate role in a relationship and am free to let others be fully responsible for playing theirs.

5. I overstep my authority when I feel I need to control people. By sharing power and relinquishing control, my trust in others may grow— and I will be not nearly so tired from trying to hold up the whole world.

6. When I find reward in continuously being the helper, I retain power in the relationship; when I relinquish or loosen my tight grasp on the resources, other people can claim and develop resources that may rightfully have been theirs all along. Sharing power is rare. The good news of radical new possibilities for power relationships is full of promise. Do we want to claim that promise?

**Dialogue**

Discuss in a trustworthy environment a concrete problematic relationship.

1.  What are the power issues in this struggle?
2.  What radical good news could turn this relationship around?
3.  How can each party relinquish some control?
4.  What could each give to this shared task?
5.  Envision alternative ways the parties could energize each other.

## Conclusion

In all arenas of life, people will continue to escalate power struggles. Most people expect one of only two responses: use every means to win, or give in to losing. We have the opportunity to reshape the struggle entirely. Within church walls and within the worlds in which we live day to day, we have the opportunity to change the way we see and use power. "Give peace a chance," the saying goes. Give resurrection and reconciliation an opportunity!

In different forms the struggles surrounding commitment, worth, pressure, and power appear in everyone's life. You may name other struggles as paramount. All relate back to questions of identity and meaning and community as we as people of God live in the world. Where in the world are we? Even in the midst of the struggle, before we have answers to—or even the shape of—the questions, we can remember and reflect on the fact that God is already in the world. Working from that perspective may reshape our questions.

PART 2

# *What in the world is God doing?*

God has been "doing," has been working in the world from all eternity to this very moment. What if for a twinkling God would withhold divine power and love from the universe? The resulting chaos would be indescribable!

Imagine the undoing of creation by reversing parts of Genesis 1 (authors' paraphrase):

> Then God no longer said, "Let us make humans in our image, after our likeness."
>
> And God no longer said, "Let the earth bring forth living creatures," and the creatures were not made.
>
> And God no longer said, "Let the waters bring forth swarms of living creatures." And there were no longer fish in the sea or birds flying.
>
> And God no longer said, "Let there be lights in the firmament of the heavens," and there was no sun, or moon, or stars.
>
> And God no longer gathered the waters together to be seas, or the land to be land.
>
> And God no longer said, "Let there be light."
>
> And the Spirit of God no longer moved over the face of the waters. And there was no darkness. There was no form or void, no earth. God was not creating the heavens and the earth. There was no beginning.

Such an exercise reminds us that God's grace continues to surround the world. In the ordinary round of daily affairs, you and I trust that God is upholding and sustaining the world and continuing to restore creation.

To be loved and saved by Christ—that is the wondrous message of the Gospel. We weak and helpless and often rebellious creatures need Christ's redemptive tenderness and firmness to be made whole. What if John 3:16 read: "God didn't love the world so God did nothing"? We would be hopeless and desperate; we would lose our moorings. And we would feel terribly alone, for it is only in Christ that we are truly brought together. In the ordinary world of daily affairs, you and I trust that Christ is knitting and weaving us together and continues to connect us with one another.

Through a resounding declaration or a still, small voice, the Holy Spirit continues to guide and direct us. When we stray or grow weary on our journeys, the Holy Spirit gives new energy and focus. One more negative spin on a Scripture: If Christ had said, "I will not send the Comforter to you," or if the Spirit hadn't come on Pentecost, how in the world would we be? In the ordinary world of daily affairs, you and I trust that the Holy Spirit surprises us, comforts us, and brings life, abundant life, to each of us.

The next three chapters describe how the work of the Creator God (chapter 5), Jesus Christ (chapter 6), and the Holy Spirit (chapter 7) permeates our lives.

CHAPTER 5

# Working in the World with Us

"Where was I? Where was God?" This is the title printed across the top of the worksheet. Below these are three times: Monday 9:00 a.m., Friday 8:00 p.m., and Sunday 11:00 a.m. Down the left-hand side of the page are three questions: Where was I? What was I doing? What was God doing in that place?

As participants thought about where they were at 9:00 a.m. on Monday and what God was doing in that place, they articulated responses, some quickly, some more hesitantly: "God was guiding me as I began my job"; "God was healing my illness"; "God was saving people"; and so on.

The probing went deeper: "God was keeping the creation alive"; "God was working through me to keep food growing"; "God was working through me to keep the accounts at the bank in good and accurate order."

On Friday night: "God was making the world more enjoyable as I relaxed with my family"; "God was refreshing me as I played tennis"; "I could sense God's presence deeply as I visited a friend in the hospital."

Listening to one another's experiences, the group soon questioned whether God's presence is more real at worship or more real in the ordinary times of the week. To be at the communion rail, to witness a baptism, to hear the Gospel, or to receive the promise of forgiveness of sin is meaningful and necessary. The presence of God's grace at the bank, on the tennis court, at home, or at the hospital is often surprising and sometimes life-changing.

Then someone remarked, "Maybe our problem is that we are dividing our activities into sacred and secular. But that's not the way life is. We know down deep that God is with us at all times and in all places."

To separate the God of Sunday from the God of Monday is to ignore that all the earth is the Lord's. We do not have two separate worlds, faith and daily life, as if there were two entities, God and world. We do not have two separate lives, the spiritual and the remainder. In fact, faith commitment is frequently so entangled in daily activities that we do not know where one begins and the other ends.

A man who had been silent felt compelled to speak: "You make it all sound so great. Last Monday I was at a meeting deciding which employees to lay off at the end of the week."

A woman added, "I didn't want to speak. I wish I hadn't gone to church last Sunday. After our ten o'clock service, we were in the parking lot rehashing the recent church council meeting. The backbiting was embarrassing."

What in the world is God as Creator doing? And what part do we play? The group dared to share. They wanted to know.

### Reflection

1. Where were you last Monday at nine o'clock? Friday evening at eight? Sunday morning at eleven?
2. What were you doing there? What was really going on?
3. What were you feeling?
4. Who or what was not there?
5. What was God doing there?

## We Are in God's Hands

One could conclude that it's a bit presumptuous to try to know what God is doing in the places we live and work. If we really knew, we would be God. God works through us and within us and around us in ways we do not see or often understand, and sometimes God works in spite of us. God's works are too great and unfathomable to be reduced to a worksheet.

But such reflection, especially together, opens us to a deeper awareness of God's being at work in all corners of the earth, all parts of daily life. The questions deepen, too, for God is indeed unfathomable, God's ways unsearchable. Still people profess a trust that God is at work in the world around them, in their places of employment, at their breakfast tables with their shared joys and quarrels, in decisions on how to care for the earth, in political processes. God creates not only Earth's hydrogen and rain, but also communications and commerce. God creates not only nature, but also human interaction. The Creator's life-sustaining power, Christ's redemptive love, and the Holy Spirit's guiding wisdom are around and within us.

The old spiritual has it right: "God's got the whole world in His hands." Christians believe the created world is not a lower order of being but the instrument of divine goodness. When God now chooses to be revealed, God does so in and through the creation itself. The finite is capable of revealing the infinite. God is thoroughly alive in the world.

A good God caringly creates an ordered existence. Believing that, in the midst of personal and communal chaos, takes trust. In a world of volitional or random violence, one is tempted to blame others, invent an enemy, or blame God. It's hard to believe the world is still in God's hands. But God didn't just wind up the world to let it run down.

The Creator God never disappears or resigns or is separated from us. In our despondency we are tempted to separate ourselves—from God, from each other, from the world—or to compartmentalize our lives in order to cope. We need not isolate ourselves, for this God is still connecting and connecting our worlds. We can know from Scripture that God's love encompasses compassionate steadfast love in the midst of all the world.

> But you, O Lord, are a God merciful and gracious, slow to anger and abounding in steadfast love and faithfulness. (Ps. 86:15)

Know God holds us still, in the midst of the doubts. Seek out someone you trust; share your disappointment, even your despair. Ask for and listen for a word of hope. Things may not get easier, but God does still live and care.

## Meet Mitch

My most fundamental religious experiences do not happen in church. Rather, they happen in the context of my marriage and family life. I honestly do not think church leaders understand this. My spouse and children channel God's love to me more often than do the liturgy or other church institutions.[1]

1.  How does this statement represent your own sentiments?

2.  What is true and not true for you here?

Every aspect of life from growth to death, from laughter to language, is within God's creative domain. As one probes the meanings of the questions "Why do we grow?" and "Why is laughter part of our humanity?" the inquiry inevitably moves into spiritual dimensions and confirms the connectedness of God's world. The connections do not have to be hauled in from the outside; such dimensions are integral to the phenomenon itself. The way to God is not first of all up to the heavens, but rather down to the depths of life. The question, "Should I connect faith and life?" is as absurd as, "Should the fish be in the pond?" The point is not whether, but how—how to become more fully aware of the connections between faith and life.

### Discussion

Walk with a friend and converse about ordinary, everyday things.

1.  Share with each other one distressing and one refreshing event in the past twenty-four hours.
2.  Ask each other how you connect these events to your faith.

3. Make a commitment to meet at a specific time again soon to follow up on your discoveries about each other and God's creative work in your lives.

## We Are in God's Hands

The world is the arena for our work with God. The seemingly ordinary and mundane world in which women and men cultivate fields, design computer programs, empty bedpans, and vacuum carpets—this world is God's creation; it is where the people of God are participating in the ongoing and interdependent work of God's creation. We miss the mark when we insist that people share and show their faith only through church-related work during the week. God's people are engaged in every imaginable arena, and God is at work through their labors, their care, and their concern.

God is at work in our lives, and we are God's hands despite our ambiguity and confusion. Our deceitfulness distorts our vision; our mixed priorities and motives confound our commitment to Christ. Actually we are quite capable of blocking God's good will for God's creation. Much goes wrong in life, for the world is broken and sinful. We more quickly give up on the world and each other than God does. Our very hopelessness must frustrate God's plans to use us as God's instruments for re-creation.

Is it human hopelessness that causes us to grab what we can? If people will not care for creation, if justice is thwarted, then why should I bother? Perhaps I should just take care of my yard, find a little happiness, and leave it there. We reason that it's hard enough getting our own lives together, much less collectively cooperating to be God's communal hands to care for the world. People frustrate God's plans as much out of our malaise as malice because we look around and don't believe that people will cooperate enough or that justice will win out. And too often we blame the resultant chaos on God.

In the midst of the brokenness and the blame, the God of Hope and Life who is Love comes to call the run-aways to be partners and colleagues, to participate in the care and nurture of our life together as humankind in creation. By recognizing ourselves as instruments of God, as vehicles of God's grace, as part of Christ's body alive and working in the world, we begin to be aware of what our mission in life is. Mission, as John Taylor, former bishop of Winchester said, is finding out what God is doing in the world and doing it with God.

## Meet Donny

Young Donny lived on the side street around the corner from the church. He was more adept at destruction than construction. One day he was apprehended pulling out by the roots the flowers around the church building. Dirt yet falling from his fingertips, with a line he had practiced often in his ten years, he automatically responded, "I didn't do it." Well, obviously he had. After the confrontation broke through Donny's denial and he was assured he would come to no bodily harm, Donny's apprehender invited him to help replant the flowers, from seeds. The two worked together the rest of the summer. This task took time and patience. No hot-house transplants! Donny did help plant, probably because the alternatives were not good, but also because he felt needed. He watched the plants grow to the end of the season, when he was invited to pick them—by the stem—to take them home.

1.  What changed in this story?

2.  Are you more like Donny or the apprehender or both? Why?

One of the best ways to find out what God is doing in the world is to begin inductively and concretely. Start where you are! What challenged you last week? What haunted you? What sustained you and gave you joy? At what points and in what ways did your daily living intersect with your Christian faith? How do the words and feelings of your daily living (pressure, tension, competition, success, compromise, conflict) intersect with the language of faith (prayer, discipleship, confession, forgiveness)? Yesterday what did you experience that spoke of cross and resurrection? What will it mean to live by grace tomorrow?

## The World Wants to Live Creatively

We live at a strange time. The Cold War has been over for some years, yet since then the incidence of war and terrorism has risen and private militia are stockpiling weapons. U.S. business transports raw goods half-way around the world to Taiwan and ships back clothing so Americans can purchase it inexpensively, yet we cannot figure out or do not have the will to distribute food equitably so that all can live. We can fax a message to China and receive another from Cameroon within three minutes, yet we cannot understand the world view of our neighbors, whether they are thirty thousand miles or three blocks away. Violence reigns, but people persist in wanting to live. People work as a community when flood waters rise; they ask, "Why did it take so long for us to get to know one another?" The world hungers for creative ways to live together.

Although human problems will never totally be solved, at least without inventing others more complex, God's hands are still at work in the world. We are already part of God's intricate work of creation and re-creation. From time to time news magazines break away from the fascination with disaster to report more positive news: Granted, the world's problems are depressing and overwhelming, but there's a gradual, quiet entwining of a spirit of creativity and community that joins people with longstanding differences in a common cause.

More than 40 percent of first-year college students are involved in some kind of voluntary activity. Intergenerational volunteerism—old helping young and young helping old—is growing rapidly. Communities small and large have begun projects that identify key problems, set specific attainable goals, celebrate victories, and create new communal traditions. Such endeavor in the midst of destruction testifies not to the absence of a Creator or to the defeat of God, but to the fact that God lives and reigns in spite of and in the midst of the world's darkness.

Christians know that even such creative efforts will eventually be plagued with ulterior selfish motives, but a sign of hope is promise enough that we were created by a God who designed people for diversity and interdependence. The Creator God's love can be known only through the darkness of Christ's cross and the surprise of the resurrection, but it will be known.


**Action**

Take time, maybe just ten minutes a day at first (better yet, do this with a friend), to:

1.  Watch for signs (on the street, in the news, at a meeting) in yout community of God's creating power at work.
2.  See (and admire) the hands at work in your community.
3.  Listen, too, for the deeper despair.
4.  Envision, then initiate or energize places for people to gather in community to explore creatively solutions to common problems.

CHAPTER 6

# *Bringing Us Together*

We live amid struggle and conflict. From within and without, struggles with doubts, guilt, stress, power, loneliness, and . . . more often overwhelm us. Why get out of bed in the morning if the day ahead is just one struggle after another? The struggles may lead to opposition and outright conflict. It must take "faith," we are told, to face these struggles and others, even those of which we are not yet aware. Faith in what and in whom? Faith in Jesus Christ, whose birth, life, death, and resurrection give us forgiveness and new life now and forever.

Personal faith is surely a comfort, but we may still feel isolated and disconnected from other people and their struggles. "Faith," in this society at least, is a private affair. That's not surprising because freedom of religion can mean that religion is relegated to the private sphere. When things become difficult, we return to, lean on, a personal belief in a personal God. In media interviews or daily conversation, we hear testimony: "God kept me going"; "I had God with me"; or, "God kept me safe." Hardly noticed is the incongruity: If God saved me because God loves me so much, what about the one who didn't make it? If God was on my side, what about the person on the other side who professes faith in the same God? A basic belief in rugged individualism, the competitive market, and freedom as pursuit of personal happiness, combine to underscore religion as "my God helping me get ahead."

The struggles and tensions in our lives usually are rooted in a lack of connection. Family conflict, problems where we work, violence within our neighborhoods and the country, international misunderstandings leading to terrorism or war—all of these flow from our inability and unwillingness to relate fully and deeply to one another. Sin and evil have sometimes been described as the disjunction between God and human beings. We separate and isolate and break apart that which is intended to be together. Christ's victory is not simply for individual salvation; Christ has restored the relationship between us and God, reuniting us and creating the body of Christ still active in the world.

### Reflection

1.  Take some time to name the struggles and conflicts due to a lack of connection that eat away at you daily.
2.  Name also some tensions in the broader society that trouble you deeply.
3.  What are the basic problems in those struggles? Why is it so hard to resolve the problems?
4.  Why do we have the propensity to entangle ourselves all over again?

## Beyond a God to Save Only Ourselves

Conflicts threaten all of our relationships. When I quarrel with my spouse, I am affecting my marriage. If I confront my supervisor, I may be jeopardizing my job. Within our country, controversies over priorities and discord about strategies are always with us. If our nation attempts to stop conflicts in other parts of the world, disagreements about that policy surface both at home and abroad.

In the midst of the tensions and conflict, God is at work in the world to reconcile the alienated. The "God will help me win" approach is shortsighted. God does love me personally, but God's designs are greater than my personal faith. God weeps over the ways we continue to hurt one another. The God who created us for interdependence, who has been patient and steadfast in our unfaithfulness to one another and to God, entered the world of our wars so that right relationships might be restored.

God is at work bringing us together not so that some might win and others might lose, but so that winning is no longer the goal. Had it been, Christ's victory over death, the powers of evil, and the grave might have been chalked up as Jesus' personal victory. But the angel in the garden told the women to go and tell the others that Jesus had been raised from the dead and to meet him in Galilee (Matt. 28). Jesus' resurrection is about reunion, re-uniting us with God and with one another.

At the tomb an angel asked the women why they were looking for the living among the dead (Luke 24:5). The resurrected Jesus appeared to the disappointed followers on the way to Emmaus and ate with them (Luke 24:13-32). Jesus later told Peter, "Feed my lambs . . . tend my sheep" (John 21:15-17). esus' resurrection is about life, about gathering us together with himself in the middle, about the intimacy of being fed and feeding one another.

The Emmaus disciples returned to Jerusalem and told the others that they had seen Jesus. Even when Jesus stood right among them, they still had doubts. Jesus opened their minds to understand the Scriptures and called them to proclaim repentance and forgiveness in Christ's name (Luke 24:33-48). Resurrection is about being called to reach out with words and actions of reconciliation.

God's victory is life over death. It makes former enemies into life-giving communities. By the end of the second chapter of the Acts of the Apostles, the Christian community after Pentecost is described: "All who believed were together and had all things in common" (Acts 2:44). They broke bread together and praised God, and the faith community grew. The Acts of the Apostles, the New Testament epistles, and church history go on to show us all kinds of ugly struggle. Even so, we need not fear the struggle will kill the body of Christ. Resurrection is about liberation from fear and freedom to be.


**Reflection**

1. Read the accounts of Jesus' resurrection and postresurrection appearances (see Matt. 28; Mark 16; Luke 24; John 20-21). Compare and contrast them.
2. What themes of resurrection hope for bringing us together do you find in these passages?

## Congregations Experiencing Pain and Promise

"A struggling congregation"—these words reflect the reality we often
experience. Struggling to survive, struggling to maintain itself, struggling with brokenness and conflict, a congregation can flounder and lose
its way. Although congregations are places of great joy, comfort, and
strength, the church has myriad conflicts, sometimes more than other
communities. Personality differences with the pastor, cliques, opposition
to change, disagreements about budgets or hymns—all these and more
persist within most congregations.

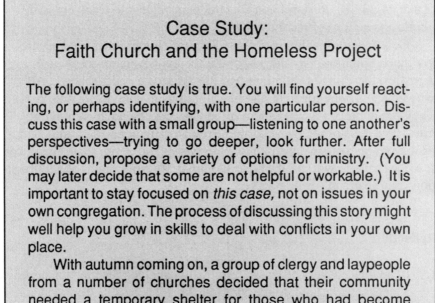

### Case Study:
### Faith Church and the Homeless Project

The following case study is true. You will find yourself react-
ing, or perhaps identifying, with one particular person. Discuss this case with a small group—listening to one another's
perspectives—trying to go deeper, look further. After full
discussion, propose a variety of options for ministry. (You
may later decide that some are not helpful or workable.) It is
important to stay focused on *this case,* not on issues in your
own congregation. The process of discussing this story might
well help you grow in skills to deal with conflicts in your own
place.

  With autumn coming on, a group of clergy and laypeople
from a number of churches decided that their community
needed a temporary shelter for those who had become
homeless. Their small city of forty thousand had undergone
much change in recent years. People released from a nearby
prison and a drug-treatment center had been staying in the
area rather than returning to the metropolitan areas from
which they had come. They saw this community as a place to
put their lives back together and make a fresh start. The state

and county had tried their best to meet the sudden increase in demand for social services, but with only limited success.

The ad hoc group arranged with several local congregations to provide supper, a place to sleep, and breakfast. Following breakfast, the guests would be taken downtown where they could spend the day looking for permanent housing and work. Faith Church had not been asked to provide overnight accommodations because the driving force behind the program was a priest from another parish in the ecumenical cluster. When word of the project hit the newspaper, people at Faith raised questions about their role.

Naming themselves the Homeless Project, the group hired a layperson to be coordinator. At this point Faith Church was approached, in a telephone call to the pastor, asking if the church could provide a place for the guests to stop in during the day to rest, make telephone calls, change diapers, etc. The pastor brought this request to the congregational council.

On the council was Peter, a Christian of deep faith whose commitment sometimes made him appear pushy as he encouraged others to live out their faith. Peter was a volunteer at the Area Rescue Services and served on its board; that program provided housing and training in life-skills, such as housekeeping, budgeting, and parenting, as well as job training. People assumed Peter would be in favor of the Homeless Project. He was not. Peter's experience told him that you build the day program first to give people direction. He also did not see the need for a program that duplicated the work of Area Rescue Services.

Another council member was Louise, a homemaker, mother, and Red Cross volunteer. A life-long member, she was devoted to Faith Church. If an event called for a meal or snacks, you could find Louise in the kitchen. To her it was only natural. Louise had compassion, but couldn't quite get used to what was happening in the city. She was a little leery about the Homeless Project; she didn't want people to suffer, but she also didn't want her city attracting even more people who seemed to bring crime in their wake.

Pastor Davis had been serving Faith Church just over five years. He was sent in by the bishop in the wake of a blow-up between the previous copastors. More than a few parishioners have taken their anger out on him; he has expressed the feeling that if he proposes something, it's a sure bet to be rejected.

The project coordinator, Jan, agreed to meet with the leaders from Faith Church to discuss what the daytime program would involve. Since the program had not yet started, she could not accurately project how many adults to expect—or how many would bring children. She could say that the "day-shift hours" would be from 7 a.m. to 5 p.m. A site was needed seven days a week, and the Homeless Project planned to continue the program throughout the year.

At the meeting Louise asked if this meant Faith Church would be expected to cover all the daytime hours and to provide volunteers. Jan said yes. Pastor Davis asked if other congregations could not also recruit volunteers. Jan said that she had hoped Faith's people would themselves want to help rather than bring in people from elsewhere; so essentially her answer was no. Peter asked if the coordinator would be onsite to help the guests with their search for housing and work. Jan said, "No, the guests will be on their own to do what they need to do."

The group brought their information to Faith Church for a decision.

1.   What are the issues involved in this case story?

2.   Look at this situation from the differing viewpoints of the people, e.g., Peter, Louise, Jan, Pastor Davis, congregational members, the homeless people, the custodian. What might this situation look like to each of them?

3. What are the deeper faith questions about the nature of the church and its ministry?

4. What are the options and possibilities for ministry here? What would you do?

Being Christian should make things easier, but that's not our experience and not God's promise. It's hard enough feeling tossed around in the world—morally, relationally, spiritually. Then we are discouraged even further to find ourselves embroiled in devastating battles among Christians. We may find each other, even ourselves, having learned many crafty, scheming, deceitful ways to kill each other "nicely." Our witness becomes, "See how well they hate each other," and people leave or refuse to join a congregation.

Amid all of our struggles and conflicts, God is at work in the world (including the world that is the church) to bring us together and make us whole. Some people draw a line between the church and the world, assuming one is good, the other evil; one full of dangerous people, the other full of good ones. There is no such line because the church, though blessed by God, is also a human institution. We should not be surprised when we encounter conflict inside the church walls; in fact, we could be surprised that there is not more. Our disappointment may be greater because our expectations of the church are higher.

In the midst of the conflict, God's promise that Jesus' resurrection joins us together as the body of Christ is true. God empowers us through repentance and the gift of new life to become one. We can draw on Christ's healing and reconciling work among us. Mutuality and interdependence are gifts for us to live. No words that Jesus spoke are more meaningful than "one another."

## Discussion

With one or more friends who belong to the same (or different) faith communities:

1.  Recall and discuss the pain of a conflict in your congregation.
2.  What misunderstandings linger?  What scars?
3.  Recall and tell about a time when Christ's healing reconciliation was
    a reality in your congregation.
4.  How did it come about?  How did it empower you for ministry
    beyond yourselves?

# Seven Directives to Bring Us Together

## 1. Rely on God

So simple and yet so difficult. We want to be the central players; we
want to figure out for ourselves how to escape the struggle or to resolve
the conflict. We want to impose our own rules upon the events and people in our lives. We construct layer upon layer of defenses to keep the
unexpected and the unpredictable from upsetting our carefully ordered
world.

   If we are imprisoned by the need to control our existence, we cannot
be God's person for others; rather, we are captive to the need to protect
ourselves against others and manipulate them for our own purposes. Nor
can we be agents of God's grace to a broken and hurting world. These
efforts to rely on ourselves isolate us from God and close us to the
strange and mysterious working of God in the world. To rely on God is
to trust the liberating power of Christ that frees us to become the people
God intends us to be together.

## 2. Remember Our Baptism

Each of us is called to Christ in baptism. That is the most fundamental
identity of members of the Christian community. Amid all differences of
status and title and in the midst of antagonisms, each of us is a child by
Christ's grace. The church is a community of those who have been promised forgiveness of sins and newness of life through baptism in Jesus
Christ. Such a community of believers, such a priesthood of the baptized,
lives in the awareness that through the cross we as resurrection people
are empowered to live in suffering love for our neighbor.

   What God has done in uniting us in Christ's death and resurrection
in baptism, God continues to do each moment of our lives as we face

conflicts and struggles. God has defeated the forces of evil. That does not mean that we have no more struggles, but that, beginning with the life-giving waters of baptism, Christ gives us faith and hope.

### 3. Recognize the Variety of the Spirit's Gifts among God's People

We need the variety of gifts the Holy Spirit gives to the Christian community, but sometimes those differences result in conflict. The gifts of being prophetic—urgently advocating a needed change within the congregation—may be in direct opposition to another's gift for patience or wisdom concerning how people can best be open to new ideas.

A community of Christians is a collection of gifts, a kaleidoscopic variety with the potential to bring out each person's strengths and carry each person's weaknesses. Out of the Spirit's infinite imagination comes the church's rich variety of gifts. We dare not stifle one another's gifts or hide our own. The body of Christ is healthy when all of us use our gifts to respond to others and to nurture one another for mission. Out of such oneness of Spirit and such diversity of gifts, the work of Christ is called forth.

### 4. Trust One Another

People may leave the church because of conflict more than for any other reason. People don't join a church because they see a good fight going on there. Neither will they join or stay at an apathetic church exhibiting no energy. But the opposite of destructive conflict is not boredom. It is trust. Can I trust the church? We hold false expectations when we hope to find a church in which there is no conflict, and yet we can hope for and work toward a faith community that is a place to faithfully struggle with the conflict. This calls for a trustworthy environment.

We cannot fully trust one another, particularly ourselves. God *is* love and God is trustworthy. We can confidently trust God's love, which frees us to create a trustworthy environment to live in relationship.

### 5. Encourage and Support One Another

Paul's advice is needed: "Therefore encourage one another and build up each other" (1 Thess. 5:11). In the intricate web of diverse, active, changing people, each member is called to care faithfully for the other.

We may be able to work through some of our bondage and brokenness alone with God. But when God begins to deal with us, we will ultimately need to deal with one another. In such times we confess our sin to one another and bear one another's burdens. Christ reunites us so that we become for one another the means of grace through which God brings us to wholeness. Reunion is God's gift.

## 6. Bear One Another's Pain and Suffering
In a caring fellowship in Christ, the people care for one another and for those around them. They really care! Again, in the words of the apostle Paul, "If one member suffers, all suffer together" (1 Cor. 12:26). We help to create Christian community when we enter one another's pain and become part of a fellowship of suffering. That means listening, listening very carefully. Jesus listened; he listened more than he spoke. He listened to Nicodemus; he listened to the woman at the well; he listened to the disciples and to the Pharisees. To listen to another's needs is a sign of God's grace working in our world.

## 7. Work at a Shared Vision of Mission
When struggles and conflicts fester within and among, as individual people and as members of congregations, they hinder us from being the body of Christ; they prevent us from doing what is the essential priority of individual Christians and of the church: to be in mission in the world, to share the great Good News.

When a congregation looks inward only, the result is poor morale, stress, and an obsession with maintenance. Many congregations today are so concerned about survival (where is the money coming from to continue? how can we afford a pastor?) that they lose the mission of the church to make the Gospel real.

But if we recognize and engage the larger challenge of mission, we will turn outward, reaching into the world to witness and serve and heal. We may individually go in different, even opposite, directions. We may share a vision and yet see different causes of injustice, different people in need of hope, different signs of suffering. Yet we will have been in mission together because the Christ who unites us in baptism frees us to listen and grow, in our differences, together.

(Oh, and whatever happened to the Homeless Project? Faith did vote to participate. Three years later the project is still going and has become interfaith with the Jewish and smaller Muslim communities also participating. They are now also working on broader community issues to help people grow beyond fear of one another.)

## Listen and Act

1. Picture some of the many Christians you have known. Recount their differences. How was that variety both a struggle and a gift?
2. Gather some people together who (a) are experiencing the tensions of lack of trust and (b) want to explore problems. Listen to one another; avoid putting up defenses. Going around the circle, listen to each one's fears and hopes.
3. Explore with one another each person's vision of what mission in the world means. What is central in each? How can you support one another in your common yet diverse challenges?

## CHAPTER 7

# Surprising with Spirit

It is 9:45 p.m. and the committee has been meeting in the corner room of the church basement since 7:30. Everyone is weary; some are growing in frustration with one another about the many differences in the group. Is there any way out?

And then perhaps a person sitting at the end of the table comes up with an idea, a word of hope, a new direction to take.

What has happened? Could it be the Holy Spirit among us?

Are we open to being surprised by the Holy Spirit among us? Are we doubting that the Spirit may breathe new life within us?

The Holy Spirit is indefinable; yet, by suggesting several characteristics of the Holy Spirit, we may add at least a footnote to the ongoing attempt to know the Spirit and particularly how the Spirit is working in the world.

## The Presence of the Spirit

The first characteristic is that the Holy Spirit manifests itself by a presence moving among us and, most of all, within us. At the very foundation of the world, the presence of the Holy Spirit was moving on the face of the deep. Into a universe of chaos, something began to move. Above our void and barren planet, something was "hovering." There the Spirit was already, sitting on this egg of the earth, brooding and waiting for it to burst into life. The imagery of the Spirit as a bird, particularly as a dove, expresses freedom and gentleness. Later, at the Incarnation, the Spirit played the role of lover and life giver. The Spirit continues to strengthen us in deep love and to breathe life into our fragile and broken world.

A perception that arrives unexpectedly may find its source in the Holy Spirit. Surprise often marks the tempo of the Spirit; it may be the flash of insight that illumines us. By contrast, when a situation unfolds slowly, we tend to become habituated to it; we have time to explain it, to make room for it in our sense of the normal. But many of the situations that will be experienced as spiritual will themselves be quick at the crucial point. *Celebrate,* with its root in *quickness (celer),* suggests that the Holy Spirit is in a state of perpetual motion. The Spirit hovers and swoops, flits, and often moves with looseness and surprise. The Spirit is nothing, if not on the move.

The Holy Spirit is not only a presence to enliven, but also a presence to calm, to comfort, a presence to abide with us, as Jesus said, "I will pray the Father, and he shall give you another Comforter, that he may abide with you forever" (John 14:16 KJV). The Greek word translated as *comforter* is *paraclete,* meaning "one called alongside to help." The Spirit is a helper who calms our restless fears and who takes up our cause when we need help. The Spirit guides us in the paths on which we should walk and gives us great peace. In the quietness of a funeral service, the calming presence of the Holy Spirit sustains us. Thus both in firm and gentle ways, the Spirit provides direction for our lives.

## Grace is Amazing!

We sometimes use the word *grace* to describe the workings of God through the Holy Spirit in our lives and in the world around us. *Grace:* that's the most important word in God's relationship with us, God's unconditional love in Christ Jesus coming to us through the Holy Spirit. Not sin, not judgment, but grace! That's the foundation and frame of our relationship with God, with others, and with ourselves. The promise and reality is that in my unworthiness and many failures, the free gift of God's love is always there. The Spirit creates faith in our hearts to trust God's love. To pray and share the promise that each of us receives the undeserved and unearned love of God—that is amazing! And that is what grace is—the undeserved, unearned, generous saving love of God that flows freely and spontaneously and abundantly.

We are surrounded by grace. We bask in it. We live in it, as a fish in water, without really being aware of it. The phrase is true: We live by God's grace!

Grace is not simply a passively receiving from God; the Spirit empowers to grow in grace, to become more and more responsive to that amazing grace. To serve and to listen and to support and to encourage one another in response to God's graciousness—that has been, is, and continues to be what the presence of the Holy Spirit urges us to do.

The Spirit is not *above* us, as is the Father. The Spirit was not *among* us in the flesh as was the Son. But the Spirit is *in* us. The Spirit moves incognito and is revealed in a hidden inwardness, a presence within us. The Spirit's presence is also working within others, uniting us in the Spirit. Most of all, the Spirit is acting through us in life, helping us to change what needs to be changed in the world.

**Reflection**

1.  Name some images—or action words (verbs)—that you associate with the Spirit's action.
2.  How has the Holy Spirit surprised you, brought you to faith?
3.  How has the Holy Spirit given you help, comfort?
4.  What new idea or calling is the Spirit stirring within you?
5.  How have you seen the Spirit bringing new life, in small or grand ways, within your congregation?
6.  What new images and actions now come to mind?

## Blowing in the Wind

A second characteristic of the Spirit is in its connotations relating to *breath* and *wind*. The Holy Spirit, of course, blows where it lists, or, as we might say today, "when and where it pleases." The term *spirit* is based, linguists say, on the Hebrew word *ruach*, defined as "wind." Indeed, the Holy Spirit blows when and where it wants.

One writer has described the breath of the Almighty, the Holy Spirit, as

•   the "wind" of *creation*, fashioning the universe from chaos.

- the "wind" of *animation*, giving Adam his physical and spiritual life.
- the "wind" of *perception*, allowing us to hear the gentle breezes of God's voice.
- the "wind" of *direction*, gently guiding in the paths we should go.
- the "wind" of *revitalization*, quickening and renewing us every day, giving us strength for the journey.[1]

The Spirit of God not only is the planet's lifeline for survival (the Spirit keeps on restoring creation), but it is also the power that transforms death into life. The Spirit creates faith to believe the unbelievable—that there is life after death.

Such vitality and transformation gives us deep and lasting hope. As Paul writes, "And hope does not disappoint us because God's love has been poured into our hearts through the Holy Spirit that has been given to us" (Rom. 5:5). Such hope leads to renewal and celebration.

The Holy Spirit asks us to get into the spirit of the thing. The essence of the Holy Spirit is party loving—like the shepherd who finds one lost sheep and then calls his friends and neighbors together to help him rejoice. Like the village woman who comes across one little coin and invites everyone to share the happiness. Like the prodigal's father who brings out the best robe and ring and the fatted calf and wants all to participate in the festivities of a lost child returned home. The party will be held; as J. B. Phillips translates the father's call to exuberance in Luke 15:32: "But we *had* to celebrate and show our joy."

Pentecost, aptly celebrated when "June is busting out all over," marks the day when people were first filled with the Spirit. Exuberantly energized, they were accused of drunkenness, that is, of being overwhelmed by the spirit of spirits. When the Spirit fills us, we can exhibit and feel a mild insanity—a slight zaniness. As the Benedictine Breviary exhorts us: "*Laeti bibamus sobriam/Ebrietam Spiritus . . .* [Let us joyfully taste of the sober drunkenness of the Spirit]." The enthusiasm of all those at Pentecost who had tongues of fire above their heads amazed everyone; in the root sense of *enthusiasm,* they were possessed by a god. Both wind and fire—the invisible and the visible—filled the place. The Spirit moved like a heavenly whirlwind; each person was overflowing with the Holy Spirit.

The Pentecost joy was one of breathful and vital energy, a sheer riot that left them rolling in the aisles. And the result of all this spontaneity was the formation of a new community:

All who believed were together and had all things in common; they would sell their possessions and goods and distribute the proceeds to all, as any had need. Day by day, as they spent much time together in the temple, they broke bread at home and ate food with glad and generous hearts, praising God and having the goodwill of all the people (Acts 2:44–47).

The new community is one based on unity and open to possibility and adventure.

## In the Community of the Spirit

This leads us to a third characteristic of the Holy Spirit:  community. The Holy Spirit breaks down barriers and social and economic differences, creates unity and community, and assumes that society must be made to work—that we can somehow learn to live together. The climate of the Spirit closes the social distance between the rich and the poor. The Spirit wills us finally to be one. Separation and alienation from self and society and God is transformed into the congruity of community. The Spirit joins and knits us together.

Many of us have felt a deep sense of oneness while singing a hymn in a worship service. A relationship of unity and love is the presiding expression of the Holy Spirit, for we are joined together in the Spirit. The Spirit is a communal gift. We don't each have a little spirit following each of us around to help us out. The Spirit is about reunion, bringing us together when space and time and our own apathy have separated us. Christ is alive in the world and walking about in and through us by the Spirit's power, by the Spirit's making us one, even when we are separated from one another. The very phrase "to be in the Spirit" implies that we are in the Spirit together. The Spirit's power is real, but often unrealized in our daily life together.

## What is the Holy Spirit doing here?

One sorrowful day a congregation voted to dissolve itself. For fourteen years they had struggled with leadership that did not minister to the needs of the community. Many times the laity had tried to address the issues, but still people left. Even though one of the voters felt the congregation was doing the best thing by closing its doors, it left an ache in the pit of his stomach. "What is the Holy Spirit doing here?" he asked.

As a church the people had listened, probed, and supported one another in a difficult decision. They had struggled together on how to respond to the call of discipleship, and it was leading them in multiple directions. Twenty members had left to join a nearby congregation.

The remaining people do not know what the future holds. Will the judicatory sell the property or start over with a new mission developer? But they do know that they were not able to continue being responsible in paying their bills. They do know that the hurt and pain between the pastor and congregation was too overwhelming for any foreseeable reconciliation.

A woman said, "The struggles were on the table and we, together with God's help, had to address them. I saw the pain in the eyes of others. I heard the struggles in all the voices. It didn't make it any easier, but I also knew that I was not alone . . . ."

1.  How would you describe the Holy Spirit working within this situation?

2.  What difficulties within your own congregation still need the  healing power of the Holy Spirit?

3.  What concrete ways does the love of the Holy Spirit characterize the life of your congregation?

4.  How is the Spirit still yearning for unity within and among faith communities?

## The Spirit Frees Us

A fourth characteristic of the Holy Spirit is evident in 2 Corinthians 3:17: "Now the Lord is the Spirit, and where the Spirit of the Lord is, there is freedom." Living in the Spirit results in a community of freedom. Such freedom is not unrestrained license. Freedom of any kind exists only in a relationship of mutual love and commitment, of giving and receiving, of energy and joy and breath and life.

The Holy Spirit empowers us, not in the sense of power over, but power with. The Spirit's power is unlimited; that means we need not be afraid of the other person being empowered to serve. Your being empowered by the Spirit, and not by some other oppressive power, empowers me with Christ's love to serve.

"Behold, how these believers love one another," was a common observation about the early church. Out of this love of Christ and with one another, they were ready to serve others in the name of Christ. The work of the Holy Spirit is not only inward, but also outward. The Holy Spirit directs, prepares, and strengthens us for service. To live in the Spirit does not mean simply to enjoy a spiritual "high," but to be deeply committed to be Christ's person wherever we are.

And we, like those first believers at Pentecost, are in the same Spirit, the Spirit that on Pentecost was regarded by many as whimsical, surprising, capricious, reckless, fantastic, irreverent, even blasphemous. Nothing as vital as the Holy Spirit can be boxed, wrapped, and tied up. The Holy Spirit will keep right on blowing where it wishes to. It is the wind of freedom, the freedom of God.

There is no place where the Spirit's presence cannot be. We are to be open to the grace of God. We proclaim it loudly and clearly: Our future, living in God's grace by the Holy Spirit, is wide, wide open.

### Challenge

1. What barriers in your life have been broken down by the Holy Spirit?
2. How are you open to the work of the Holy Spirit?
3. What is the Spirit trying to unleash in your life? In your congregation?

# PART 3

# How in the world do we keep connected?

"How in the world . . . ?" So begins many a sentence in the course of a day's conversation. How in the world do you do that?" "How in the world do you stay in your church . . . marriage . . . job?" "How in the world am I going to understand?" We are finite, frustrated, hope-filled, hungering people who in the midst of struggle want to link our faith with daily life. Chapters 8, 9, and 10 describe concrete ways to stay connected, make a difference, and hold each other accountable.

Grade school children take a walk around the block, hand in hand, led by a teacher who helps them learn to look and listen. Adults scurry to catch the mass transit, to beat the morning rush hour on the expressway, or to wipe the jam off Jenny's face because "it's our turn to drive the carpool." We may nostalgically hunger for that experience we had as children when we were invited to look and listen. As busy adults, we need to find ways really to see and hear the world in which we now live. By sharpening our perception, by asking questions, we can more clearly see the people to whom we are already connected. Perhaps God is calling us to walk with one another in healthy interdependence.

For most of us, watching the world is not enough. We want to make a difference in and for the world. To do so we need to discover ways to connect with one another and to share power so we don't kill each other. We can develop strategies that use the community's gifts and multiply ministry.

Faith communities want to make a difference, too. And yet congregations find amazing ways to stunt their own growth and to stew in their own conflict. The Gospel we proclaim is a victory of life over death. That means our mission is not to compete or conquer but to liberate and reunite.

But who's going to make sure we keep on task? Our leaders? Too often we think of leaders as parents to goad as well as guide. No wonder no one wants to lead. The scenario can be deadly. When we leaders grow frustrated begging, we lower our expectations. The only role for childlike parishioners is to rebel by not showing up, withholding their offerings, or getting rid of the pastor. The way out of the downward spiral of fatigue and frustration is not through authoritarianism where absolutes are promised but through mutual accountability, through, paradoxically, expecting not less but more of each other.

What if congregational members were connected in mutual account-ability? What if we began our connection with where we are in the world? Christians want to make a difference in the world and really want someone to ask how . . . in the world . . . it's going. By "walking around the block" with one another, we can grow in skill to care for one another within the congregation and also to hold one another in mutual accountability as we discern how in the world to be in mission.

CHAPTER 8

# *Walking around the Block*

How long has it been since you walked around the block? That may not be literally possible. Perhaps the street where you live doesn't have sidewalks. Maybe there are no blocks; you live on a farm or in a subdivision or on a street with no outlet, or maybe you simply "can't get there from here." No matter where we live, we need to see clearly our own world as well as to appreciate the view from the other side of the street, for we each live with our own view of the world. Whether a walk around the block means a city block, a farm section, or the global community, we need to go out to listen and look and feel and really see what's going on.

Many people feel totally disconnected from their own neighborhoods, or they live compartmentally, keeping relationships from the different arenas of their lives separate. How do we know where in the world we are? And what will help us connect with others? We need to walk with one another, to ask others how they see things, and then to listen and learn.

**Action**

Take time out—no simulation here.

1.  Go outside and walk. Or climb into your car and drive, with no particular destination in mind, no appointment to keep.
2.  Take time to look at your world as though you were seeing it for the first time.
3.  Stop here or there for a closer look.

Did you really do it, or are you reading this paragraph, having simply skipped over the above? (You can mentally walk around the block if need be.) Which direction did you turn? What did you see? Who was there? What thoughts and feelings ran through your mind?

## A Walk around the Community of Morrison

As one drives around Stevens County (all names have been changed), the rolling hills and rich farmland witness to the fertile river valley. Morrison, though not a county seat or even a retail center, is larger than the towns around. Henning, Lake Mills, and Mossrock all lie in the shadow of Morrison.

Family groups interconnect. People reach out to one another with care in formal and informal ways. These people haven't needed outsiders for survival. There are "local ideas" and "outsider ideas." Considering the area's agriculture-based economy, the language spoken here is farming and seasons. This warm, June day is in haying season—followed by detassling, and later harvest season.

Unless you stay in the family business whether that's in town or on the farm, if you leave for college, you probably won't come back, particularly if you receive training beyond what the local economy can use. There are no chain stores here. A few years ago a nationwide convenience store wanted to come in; that prompted the gas station owner, real estate agent, insurance agent, grocery store, and telephone company to get together and open their own highway-convenience grocery store. Morrison is on Highway 72, the old road to the state capital. There's still quite a bit of through traffic.

Every year, the first week in June, the volunteer fire department sponsors a carnival. Morrison has community pride. A growth group works to bring in new industry, and the town has been able to keep the grade school, junior high, and high school together.

There being no postal delivery, the "city gate" is the post office, especially between 8:30 and 9:30 each morning when the mail is put out. People linger and talk. Later in the day small groups will meet informally but predictably at Jonathan's Cafe—the older women after mass, then the Lions, and then the retired folk.

Class reunions are held at the cafe, as are wedding anniversaries and funeral meals. This public place is not closed to the public during such private affairs; there's simply a section beyond the salad bar where "private" groups meet. The lines between public and private are blurred in Morrison. There are two softball diamonds and almost everyone is involved in community baseball. (There are no bowling or swimming or golf facilities.) The whole town goes to school athletic events and to the plays and musicals. People know and care about one another. They become involved in elections and the blood drive exceeded its goal.

The churches mark the passages in life. Spirituality is measured in continuity, land, and the next generation. The church is seen as fortress and the keeper of continuity.

In Morrison the town whistle blows at 7 a.m., noon, and 6 p.m. The church bells ring at noon and 6 p.m. The town and the church mark the passing of time. Near Jonathan's Cafe is the library and the newspaper office. It's a weekly, and the staff doesn't go out to gather the news. The news, they expect, will come to them. It's a paper in which all can find themselves, maybe even in a photo on the front page.

Whether you live in Morrison or Milwaukee, whether you walk around town by yourself or with others, in your own community or as a guest in another, you can focus perspective, ask, reflect and learn. Questions for reflection:

1.  Who lives here?

2.  Who is not here?

3.  Do people know each other?  What enhances or hinders such knowing?

4.  Is there a community here?  A community center?

5.  What are the images or metaphors for community or meaning-making?

6.  Is this primarily a place for life or death?  Both?

7.  What is God doing here?

Such asking, listening, and reflecting can help us understand one another, our similarities and differences, and can help us respect and cherish ourselves and one another, thereby strengthening the possibilities for healthy interaction.

## The Need for Connection

When rural communities lose farms, then the local grade school, then the grocery store and restaurant, they have lost significant ways of connecting with one another. When city neighborhoods lose their grocery store and restaurants, they too have lost significant ways for neighbors to connect with one another. Such communities may have a hard time facing the fact that they can no longer financially support a full-time pastor. When you can't have your own pastor, are you no longer a church?  In some places, a deeper and broader sense of church has enabled two, three, and sometimes five congregations to see themselves as a parish, sharing staff, resources, programs, and hope.

People's lives connect in a myriad of ways, but intersections of commerce, social life, education, and business may have little relationship to one another. Put another way, people's private and public lives may be quite disconnected. In some communities public and private are quite distinct; in others they tend to overlap. Because people need connections to make meaning in their lives, it is important to understand the connections and the gaps. By simply walking (or driving) around the area, alone or with others, we can begin to observe and map the networks, clarify how they function, and discuss how they help or hinder effective life together in the community.

Congregations provide ways for people to connect with one another and with their own pasts and futures. Such connections can provide a healthy network or an entangling web; congregations can hold one another together while also allowing new members to enter, or they can bond people so rigidly no one can move and no one can join. How permeable are the boundaries of your faith community? Can people come in? Can people see out? Where in the world is your congregation? Talk with some people in the church about its location in the community. Are you (1) in the center of things? (2) "one block off" main street literally or figuratively? (3) unknown to anyone outside the congregation?

**Action**

Together, with others in your congregation, walk (or drive) around your neighborhood.

1.  Talk to some folks on the street, at the local convenience store, mall, or real estate office.
2.  If there aren't blocks or sidewalks, go to a mall or park and look and listen.
3.  Do people here know your church exists? What is their perception of your congregation?
4.  How is the congregation connected to the community?

## Created for Community

God calls us to create community. We were created for interdependence, but have found myriad ways to remain disconnected, competitive, and dangerous to one another. Disillusioned and fearful, we separate ourselves even more, building private fortresses for homes and arming ourselves with handguns.

When Norma's family lived in the inner city of Detroit in the late 1960s, they, together with congregation members and neighbors, formed a block club. They visited everyone around a two-block area and wrote and distributed a newsletter. Simply knowing one another's names and stories helped significantly during and after the riots of 1967 and 1968. Today, thirty years later, with more guns everywhere and less trust, initiating and sustaining life-giving connections is even more needed.

We are perplexed by the escalating violence in our communities. Why are we afraid of one another? We fear going out on the streets and have come to fear a gunshot through the window killing a child in bed. Our staying inside locked doors only makes the vacant city square more dangerous. Some communities sponsor programs to "take back the night," wanting women—and men—to feel safe being outside at night. Neighbors in Concord, North Carolina, sponsored events in the park every summer night as a way to say no to drug dealers and to help people enjoy one another—to "take back the park."

Where in the world is the church? We may sing figuratively "A Mighty Fortress Is Our *Church*"—locking its doors, too. A locked, empty church building bears witness to a remote, hidden God. Faith communities can dare to open their doors if they do it together. Iglesia Lutherana San Juan Congregation in Worcester, Massachusetts, is housed in a former funeral parlor. There are no windows in the building, but the people are windows to the world. Each weekday morning young mothers gather to pursue their GED while cribs for infants surround the baptismal font in the sanctuary.

Saint Paul congregation in Clinton, Iowa, is almost under the bridge over the Mississippi. The congregation has changed its name three times; the face of the neighborhood has changed more times than that. They have remained downtown because each generation has "walked around the block" to discern the congregation's calling.

The Christian church has become as fragmented as society itself, dividing and competing and thereby neglecting a unified approach to serving its neighborhood. But there are congregations that have combined energies to proclaim the good news of life rather than becoming petrified in the midst of the escalating rate of murder and violence. The Northside Strategy Group in Milwaukee combines the resources of a dozen congregations, those in the inner city and in transition zones. All congregations remain distinctive in autonomy, budgets, staff, and style, but no one congregation ever feels alone in what could be a lonely, discouraging mission of serving its neighborhood. When Cross Church burned, while embers were still smoldering, citywide support surrounded the church community.

## Global Connections

If one listens carefully in Stevens County, one can hear deeper and broader insights during a conversation in a church fellowship hall in Morrison. Highway 72 is not a U.S. highway, but that doesn't mean the people are disconnected from main roads. It's a farming community, after all. How often do any of them get to Chicago or New York City? And yet conversation drifts beyond the state line, beyond the Atlantic and Pacific. These people have traveled to all parts of the world, on business, to visit relatives. They also know about the church in other parts of the world.

We *are* connected, as a global family, as a global economy, as political allies or enemies. Even adversarial lines are not as clear as they may once have been. A rural community in the Midwest may have more in common with a village in Central America than with megapolis, U.S.A., and more at stake in understanding rural economies around the world. In Morrison, the postmaster's daughter teaches English in Korea. The insurance agent's son married a woman from Peru; the young couple's parents are taking a year of retirement to serve as volunteer technicians in West Africa. We are connected by family, fax, and finance.

What will we do with these connections? We are aware of the ugly American phenomenon. We are aware that the U.S. is not necessarily number one in the world, nor need it be. It's almost as easy to fly around the world as to walk around the block. Allegiances are ambiguous. There's more to grapple with than we can imagine, and yet we have to do so.

To walk around the block is to travel the globe. Knowing that the God in whom we believe created all peoples both comforts and challenges us. Nothing is outside God's creative acts and care. We need not fear connecting with the world; we dare not neglect knowing and caring. A thoughtful walk around the block *is* a walk around the world.

## Concrete Strategies to Keep Connected

Together we can develop the healthy interdependence for which God
creates and to which God calls us—not only within and among religious
communities, but also in the neighborhood, community, and worldwide.
We propose these action strategies:

    1. Form a block club, not a neighborhood watch, which focuses on
keeping strangers out, but a place where people know one another and
are known so that they become comfortable and confident enough to
welcome diversity.

    2. Seek out or help shape community centers where people can
come together frequently to share daily struggles and hope.

    3. Discover ecumenical and interfaith cooperative networks; volunteer for dialogues and projects that strengthen them.

    4. Walk with others as they move through the week in activities of
business, commerce, education, leisure, and reflect together on their interconnected systems of meaning.

    5. Research the ways in which nearby communities (inner city,
suburb, and edge city; open country township and county seat) drain or
complement one another. Help form a partnership between two different
communities.

    6. Become involved in long-range planning projects locally, statewide, and nationally.

    7. Form discussion groups to help people understand the global aspects of their lives and to make decisions that contribute to peace and
justice.

    To walk around the block is to begin a journey that has no end. To
look and really see, to listen and really learn, is to avoid jumping to quick
conclusions and to be open to understanding (1) the complexity of people's lives and (2) the inevitable change in any neighborhood, even the
seemingly most stable. In Morrison, for example, the agriculture-based
economy is changing. One or both adults in the family must work fulltime in town to support the farm. Some have to drive to the next town
and take a job that is not as intellectually stimulating as farming. The
language is no longer just agriculture, and many don't have time to meet
and talk at the "city gate" post office. Their small town cannot be idyllically preserved in time. They've experienced the growing availability of
drugs and the rise in crime that characterize our society. There's a

weariness in coming to church because of multiple responsibilities. There's no more time here than anywhere else to "walk around the block." And yet—wherever we are—we must do so because to begin the journey is to become committed to continuing to walk with one another in the midst of change.

## A Personal Option:
## Walk Once More around Some Blocks from the Past

Some of us may need to go back in time and walk around some places that have blocked us personally. Norma's father died suddenly when she was eleven. With her mother and sister, she moved to another city one week later. Decades later Norma knew she needed to revisit the city of her childhood. She did, driving, walking, remembering, crying so that it would no longer hold her captive.

We can retrace our steps, at least mentally, for release from old fears, bondages that inhibit our stepping out and walking freely. What unfinished business did you leave with whom? How can revisiting those places free you to be really connected and engaged in meaningful ministry now?

## Discipleship as Connection with Christ

Jesus frequently said, "Come, follow me," and he also said, "Go your way!" What did he mean? How can we do both? By being connected to Christ in baptism and becoming members of the body of Christ, we are connected to one another in the faith. Members of the church go many directions all week long, some of them seemingly opposite directions from one another politically, economically, and philosophically. Discipleship is rooted in being connected to Christ. His words of healing and new life, "Your faith has made you well; go in peace" (Mark 5:34), empower us to be on our way and to serve in the world. (Read the women of great faith Gospel of Mark to see the juxtaposition of Jesus' invitation and empowering challenge.) On these daily journeys it is easy to become disconnected from one another and even from Christ—who calls us, but does not tether us. Connection with Christ allows us to walk all the way around the block. We are sent forth, on our particular way, to be faithful disciples connected with Christ and one another.

## Reflection

Trace your steps through a week. Perhaps even map it out.

1.    What parts of the world do your feet touch?
2.    Whom did you meet there?
3.    Whom were you following?  Whom were you leading?
4.    How do you keep connected?

Talk with someone in your faith community about this reflection. As we discuss with one another those particular experiences, we can begin to understand more fully our relationships to and in the world. As we relate those experiences to our faith, we can find strength and direction for making a difference in the world.

## CHAPTER 9

# *Making a Difference*

All of us want to make a difference in the world, and some of us go to exorbitant means to achieve immortality through our accomplishments. We want to know that we count for something, that our lives have meaning. Whether influencing a decision, erecting a building, or helping someone in need, we want to know life is changed for the better because of what we do.

A lifetime of work can be erased, however, by someone else's action, and even the tallest monuments can be toppled in a minute by forces we cannot control. How can we have taken such pride in an accomplishment that passes away in a whisper? Even if people applauded our initial efforts, how can they so quickly forget us when our work is overshadowed by someone else's achievement?

"We shouldn't do good to receive a reward or recognition," you quickly respond. No, but people do, if in subtle ways. Even so, we learn the futility of that approach to self-satisfaction in a capricious world. We know God created us for creative interdependence, to do the world's work together, but it seems so much safer not to aim very high, not to risk very much. How can I know that what I do will make a difference?

We might be inspired by stories of ordinary people whose brave actions changed things.

Take the parents of the seven-year-old American, Nicholas Green, who was killed in a drive-by shooting while the family was vacationing in Italy. Their decision to donate his organs to give life to seven people in that country touched the hearts of the Italian people and increased organ donor pledges there by 25 percent.

Consider Norma's aunt and uncle (and godparents) who, once married, decided to sit together in church—in church where men sat on one side and women on the other. They sat first on the women's side and the next week on the men's side. Soon another couple followed, and then others. Surely that story had some influence when Norma decades later sought ordination.

There's the woman who could have moved to the suburbs but didn't, committed as she was to staying with her family in the inner city to work in block clubs, to teach children and then their children in their neighborhood church. When her own sons, who lived in the midst of violence, were incarcerated, she organized transportation for other prisoners' families who didn't have cars to make prison visits.

There's the man who had to take early retirement because of mental illness. But after seeking help for himself, he then devoted the rest of his life to volunteer work in his community.

There are thousands of stories of people of faith who throughout history, often in out-of-the-way places, changed their worlds and the worlds of people for generations to come. Some people act courageously as a result of profound suffering. Some because they were on the scene at the right moment. Others make a difference through years of dedication. We may not know when which of our actions—if any—will make a difference. But we act anyway.

## Reflection

Remember someone in your own life who made a difference.

1.  What difference did this person make?  What was the motivation? Where did this person find his or her strength?
2.  What immediate consequences did the action have?  What lasting difference did it make?
3.  What effect did it have on you?
4.  Tell that story.

## The Difference that Makes a Difference

We may be modestly reluctant to tell a story about something we personally did that made a difference. Sometimes we do not even know that something we have said or done has effected some positive outcome. Few of us have enough objectivity or live long enough to have the perspective of history—to know which endeavors are ultimately significant. But our labors, our choices, our connections do have consequences.

Sometimes we err on the side of acting outrageously to try to gain recognition, but more often we deprecate ourselves, refusing to believe that we have anything to offer. Stories of saints serve only to make us feel guilty or inadequate. If others' lives are so much more inspirational, why even attempt changing the world?

We often renounce God's good and gentle will for our lives by trying to immortalize ourselves or by hiding in self-deprecation. But God in mortal flesh entered a world dancing with death so that we could be freed through forgiveness to carry the Word of life. That makes all the difference. We are reunited in Christ to build community in the midst of arguing neighbors, competitive co-workers, and "foreign" countries. In and through oppression, God frees people to free others.

## Transforming Power

Amazingly, grace-filled actions call for and call forth a transformation of people's lives and also a powerful transformation of societal goals and of power itself. The Spirit's power is unlimited, communal, and life giving. The world quantifies power. For example, if one nation gains military might, its neighbor becomes more vulnerable. If one company loses assets, its weakness is counted as gain by the competition. But the Spirit empowers in radically different ways.

The difference is an omnipotent all-powerful God who does not hoard power and did not create us to have godlike power over other people or over the world itself. Jesus, who purposely became weak, puts all principalities and powers to death, transforming life and power itself. We can claim the power of our God-given gifts and talents and use them to serve, perhaps in ways the world may never understand. But this service is a powerful servanthood that assumes we can make a difference in the world.

Ministry multiplies when we claim the unlimited power of the Spirit at work in the growing body of Christ. This may mean that a real estate firm dares to think about home-ownership differently; as an agent works in areas that others red-line, entire blocks that otherwise might be demolished could become revitalized. This probably can happen only after new partnerships are forged among zoning boards and neighborhood associations and financial institutions. In this situation the "difference" is not only in outcome, but also in method and motive and ways people walk and work together.

**Discussion**

Discuss with a few friends the power issues present in a local problematic situation.

1.  Who has the power?  Who doesn't?
2.  What previously discounted differently abled people could become human resources?
3.  Look around to see which people are not yet included and empowered. How might they see the situation differently?
4.  Brainstorm some creative ways of power sharing. Talk—and act!

## Spirituality Is Always Communal

We can't make a difference alone. Neither is the Spirit confined to one person's bedside devotions or one church's sanctuary. For some people, spirituality is having a religious experience (a difference inside the self). For others, being spiritual means modeling one's life after Jesus (a difference in lifestyle).  For some, it is seeking God's will for one's life (a difference in philosophy, values, vocation).  For yet others, it is doing Christ's servant work in the world (making a difference in society.) Each of these has validity.[1] We have been made one body in Christ, with many different elbows, knees, eyes, and ears—and different experiences of spirituality. Each of us needs to grow and exercise his or her functions. Together we can be powerfully present in a world in need.

Each of us, entering the public arena from a slightly different direction, must listen carefully to understand the other's perspective and cooperatively act for the public good. This is never easy because there are many definitions of what is good for the public. And yet, recognizing our differences in spirituality, we *are called* to make differences that are just and healthy and peace producing.

## Making a Difference: Games to Forego

Making a difference involves doing things differently. When we trust that the Spirit's power is unlimited and that spirituality is communal, we will let go of some of our "old games"; we will consciously build skills for servant leadership that can enhance our opportunities to make a difference in the world.

### 1. Claiming the Credit
The disciples were caught arguing about who would sit at the right and left hands of Christ when he comes into his glory. In response Jesus said, "You do not know what you are asking" (Mark 10:38). This scene reminds us that we have been forgiven our successes as well as our failures. To claim the credit, even under a thin veil of modesty, misses the mark. Likewise we are called to servanthood, not subservience. Servanthood in Christ makes all other perks not extra credit but excess baggage.

### 2. Sabotaging a Partner
As old jealousies creep in, we make sure that colleagues do not succeed, or at least not quickly. Have you ever been set up to fail? Have you set up someone else by neglecting to pass on the correct information or share resources? When we are desperate to make a difference at the colleague's expense, we may resort to not giving her sufficient time to do a thorough job or to complaining about him behind his back. They're all familiar ways the world works, of course, but it is not to be so among us whom Christ calls together to servanthood.

### 3. Backing into Failure
Sometimes we sabotage ourselves. It is so much easier than daring to make a real difference. We start out in the right direction, perhaps even

leading others, but, seeing where such leadership may take us, we stall on the road or slide into failure. We may even participate in a backlash movement, afraid of what the Spirit may be doing with what we or others have begun.

### 4. Creating a Mess
Sometimes we spend inordinate amounts of energy to go nowhere. Some people enjoy creating chaos. Some people believe servanthood means encouraging confusion so they can rescue. This unwillingness to go anywhere may be due to a fear of change. We need one another to find our futures. We need each other's gifts to go there creatively.

### 5. Praising toward Abdication
Surely applauding the work of partners increases their productivity. We need affirmation, but praise can also be used to distance. Real praise empowers; dismissive praise signals our own abdication of partnership. "What a fine job you are doing," as we back out of the room leaves others confused, if not resentful. "I know how to delegate" may be an appropriate sharing of roles—or it might be a way to exercise irresponsible power. There's a difference.

## Skills We Can Learn

### 1. Building on Others
Nothing is totally new under the sun, and even the most inventive among us has received insight and resources from those who walked before. "According to the grace of God given me, like a skilled master builder I laid a foundation, and someone else is building on it. Each builder must choose with care how to build on it" (1 Cor. 3:10). We are called to build with care, both recognizing those who made a difference in our lives and realizing others will come after. Carefully we build on the foundation that has been laid in Jesus Christ (1 Cor. 3:11).

### 2. Seeking Consensus
"Let's vote and get this meeting over with." The matter may be decided and voters gone home, but the issue will live on through subsequent

meetings, if not for years to come. Voting is expedient but produces winners and losers. To seek consensus takes time but may actually save time in the long run. Making a difference requires the insights of all to act with wisdom. In working for consensus consider four things: First, ask yourselves who is not at the table, not in the room. How can you assure their voices will be heard? Second, listen, not only to those who are first to speak or the loudest, but by seating people so they can see one another's faces, and by drawing out and listening to each person. Third, pray for guidance during this meeting and for the consequences of your decisions. Fourth, discern and research and ask and talk some more until consensus, not total unanimity but consensus, is reached.

### 3. Challenging toward Growth

To commiserate is kind. To rejoice with someone's growth takes courage. Even while giving help, we can be partners who look for the strengths already present in those we help. I do not wish to be helped by those who "feel so good" after they have helped me. But neither do let-them-make-it-on-their-own words help change unjust systems. We need to challenge one another at our growing edges. We can serve as midwives while our companions give birth to their own new ideas, serve as resources for one another, and finally be cheerleaders as ministry multiplies.

### 4. Finding the Opposite

Note that we did not equate "opposite" with "opponent." Some church specialists assure us that churches with like-members grow and that churches reaching out to include diverse cultures will struggle. That truth has its limitations. Even people who all look alike can bicker—out of boredom. Seeking those different from ourselves, we may be surprised by what we learn, where we can be stretched, and perhaps even, finally, what we do have in common. We need the stranger—not to increase our numbers, but to be more whole.[2]

### 5. Loving the Body

Keeping connected while we go different directions is not easy. But let's face reality: Even while staying close together, we may begin to despise one another. We may come to despise ourselves as well. In 1 Corinthians 12, one of three great biblical sections on the body of Christ (see also

Rom. 12; Eph. 4), Paul sees right through us. "If the foot would say, 'Because I am not a hand, I do not belong to the body,' that would not make it any less a part of the body" (v. 15). We will not always like those with whom we are connected; nevertheless, "Now you *are* the body of Christ and individually members of it" (v. 27, italics added). We are! Christ loved the church and gave himself for it. We are loved, and love makes a difference.

If we believe the only safe place to be together is in the sanctuary or the church basement, we will never know much about one another. We will not understand the specific ministries in which each of us is already involved. But when we realize that no place will ever be safe enough (not even a house of worship), and that any ground can be holy ground if brave people make it so, we will venture out with each other and will see unending possibilities for arenas of action in daily life.

## Reflection and Dialogue

With others, if possible, list or draw your arenas of action in the course of a week.

1.   What other people are in each of those arenas?  Do we meet some of the same people in more than one arena?
2.   Which arenas might surprise or even shock friends from another part of your life?
3.   What is your ministry there?
4.   How can others support you in that role of ministry even if their roles and arenas are quite different?
5.   What can we learn from one another?

## CHAPTER 10

# *Holding Each Other Accountable*

Dear Nelvin,

"Well, how are you?" you asked me on the phone.

I think you really want to know. We use that phrase so frequently—even when we don't want to know, don't want to bother stopping, don't even necessarily want much eye contact.

But I think you want to know. I'm better, thank you. I needed rest to recuperate from my bronchitis and also from the emotional work of some professional commitments. Sometimes it's really hard to sort out the physical from the emotional or spiritual fatigue.

Maybe that's why we need the other to ask how we are. There is something very necessary in the mutuality of it all. We are put together in the body of Christ because we can't bear to be alone; we can't bear ourselves alone even though in some ways only I can know myself, know how I am. In another way I can't bear to ask myself how I really am. I need you to ask me, to care, to help me sort out my different kinds of fatigue, illness, brokenness. We can't get a very good perspective on ourselves; I'm simply too close for any perspective at all.

And in the asking, the really asking, is a contract to hear my answer. In the asking is an invitation, an expectation that I will ask you in return: How are you? There is no one-up, one-down in such a mutual exchange. We ask each other, as greeting, as acknowledgment of the other's presence, as sign of a relationship. We question and then question some more. If the response is an easy, "Fine!" we may go on our way or move on to another subject, the weather, for example. But if the answer, in even so subtle ways, is an "I don't feel well today," we ask a follow-up question, helping the other sort out the dilemma or inviting the other to tell his or her story. We may move to offer some help. "The car won't start? I could give you a lift home."

And there is an assumption that I will ask again tomorrow, and that you will do the same.

Sincerely,
Norma


Dear Norma,

How are you doing now?

Come to think of it, there's accountability in those words, isn't there? But I guess I know that if I'm asked "to be accountable," all kinds of pink and red flags go up. I start feeling that I am losing control and that the other party is taking over. I sense a legal tone and I really resist that. But deep within, I know I am accountable to God, to my family, to my colleagues, and the list goes on and on. And as it goes on, I realize that if I'm accountable, I'm to bear responsibility for relationships. Sometimes I feel I can't bear all that.

How *are* you doing?

Sincerely,
Nelvin


Dear Nelvin,

Do you become tired of being responsible? Responsibility seems to be a hazard of adulthood. A few months ago I had a conversation with one of my adult sons. I told him it wasn't that I wanted to become irresponsible, but I often grew tired of being responsible. He replied, "You just need to wear your responsibility as joy instead of as burden."

Is it like that with you? If I think of times when responsibility becomes joy instead of burden, it's when responsibility is shared. Or when we are mutually responsible. By that I refer to more than our division of work; it's also that I know what I'm responsible for and what you are responsible for and how we are accountable to one another. We may not even be working on the same things or in the same area, but I know no one of us works alone. That may seem as if it's burdensome, but in the sharing, reciprocal interest and care replace burden and fatigue.

Does any of that resonate with you?
Yes, I am doing much better, thank you.

Sincerely,
Norma


## Accountability as Judgment

Being mutually accountable may not seem to make much sense in our society. The accountability we do know is usually a one-way hierarchical arrangement. Such accountability may be merely occasional, when the subordinate believes the authority is watching. I clean the shop when I believe the supervisor is coming by. I prepare my lessons thoroughly when we are about to have an exam. As a corrective to irregular work, we have spot checks or pop quizzes, not to solve the accountability dilemma but to increase the tension by keeping people on their toes. In a competitive society, one gains advantage by keeping the others on edge, judging them to see if they measure up.

Most of us have a vague awareness that we are mutually accountable to others. But accountability often hangs like a cloud in the air, like a parent's or teacher's voice from the past: "Be a good girl, now," or, "Careful, you'll hurt yourself." It connotes, "Be . . . or try to act . . . holy"; "Don't have fun . . . or not much anyway"; "Don't associate with . . ."; "Don't"—well, don't do much of anything.

The term *accountability* has become common in the last decade especially in business and education circles. But the term and the concept itself are not frequently used within the church. Of course, pastors and church staffs regularly write reports that are evaluated. But what if a congregation had its members account for their ministry? Would we ask a member to share how she is responding to the call in her baptism to bear witness to the Gospel within her family and in the hospital where she works? How would another member respond if he were asked what he was doing as a city council official, to raise questions of justice, such as the hiring of minority police officers? In all of these areas, how can we avoid legalism, work righteousness, and the implications of an inquisition?

## Accountability as Bearing One Another

Perhaps first of all it is necessary to be clear about what accountability means and doesn't mean. To account is to tell, to explain, to value, to furnish a reckoning, to be liable, to be responsible. To be mutually accountable is to bear with one another. The calling to bear with one another indicates there will be work going on and life—a life full of "do's" not "don'ts." To bear is to hold, to support, to sustain, to give birth to, to produce by natural growth, to drive or push. It is also to suffer, to endure. We bear when we carry someone with us in our hearts and in our minds. We are not alone; Christ is with us, we are with one another. We're in this together.

On the other hand, we are not called to game playing, to pedestal putting, to tripping each other up so we can regain our self-esteem. Mutual accountability is not "check in with the pastor." It's not the "Oh, excuse me, pastor," apology after telling an off-color joke in the pastor's presence. It's not the change of conversation when a pastor enters the room.

Pastors and staff themselves may be leery of more accountability because it may bring to mind relationships that are already tense. Often they feel like mere "paid help," as though congregational members do not grasp that these people are called by God and by the congregation to bring a prophetic as well as a pastoral word. Just as congregational members may rebel at having the pastor as "boss" of their congregational activity, so pastors become nervous when a church council acts like "boss" to the pastor. "Don't forget, who pays your salary," may be the implied response to singing too many unfamiliar hymns or changing the position of the baptismal font. One can keep one's pastor in check by showing who really holds the power of the purse strings. Each of these directions is a distortion of accountability. To counter such misperceptions, we look to the biblical witness and the call to baptism.

## Accountability as God's Promise Keeping

The Scriptures are consistent that God continues to be with God's people. God's faithfulness is the core. When God's people continually broke their promises to be faithful, God continued to make them God's people again. From the covenant in the Old Testament, through the coming of the Holy Spirit, to the early followers of Christ, to today, the sustaining interaction between God and the believing community is ongoing.

The early church followed the advice given to the gathered community at Rome: "So each of us will be accountable to God" (Rom. 14:12). The history of the first Christians is filled with inquiries of how it is going, of how the lives of the faithful, both individual people and the corporate body, are growing. The believers instructed and supported one another; they, in the words of Ephesians 4:2, "are bearing with one another in love."

Our relationship to God and to one another is continuous; the sign of baptism means that we carry Christ's name in our very being. We are given an identity; we are called by Christ's name.

We also promise. We vow, in the words of one baptismal service, to "live godly lives until the day of Jesus Christ," the expectation being that the newly baptized will "bear God's creative and redeeming Word to all the world." The question is not only how faithful people are on Sunday and in their church activities, but still more how we live as faithful Christians in our daily lives.

We must also remind ourselves that the call to baptism is to discipleship, not to volunteerism, a misused term in religious circles. Volunteerism means volition. (One agrees to do a particular task.) Such willingness is to be affirmed, but the term often carries connotations of the party being willing but less than fully competent. And we know we can't really volunteer someone else ("I'll volunteer Bob"), yet we often do so somewhat jokingly. Do we realize how that kills the sense of volition and robs us of true mutuality?

We are called to discipleship; it is not an optional responsibility. Discipleship is being responsive to God and to one another. Christians are promise keepers because they have been first of all given the promises of Christ that provide energy and strength as well as forgiveness. Flowing from the promises of Christ, the church has promises to keep being called to mission. The Great Commission is not a request or an option to consider. We are accountable to go and carry God's Word to all corners of our lives as well as to all corners of the earth.

Fundamentally, is your congregation a group of people surrounding one minister (the pastor), or is it a ministering community of Christ's people serving and accountable to God, to one another, and to the world around?

**Reflection**

1.  How can we inquire, be truly inquisitive (without being inquisitors), of the other?
2.  What concrete questions would call you to accountability?
3.  What supportive follow-through would help you? What supportive follow-through could you give to another?

# Nurturing Accountability within the Congregation

Accountability to others within the community of faith is difficult. Some feel inadequate to witness for Christ in daily life. Others are frustrated by being perceived as super-Christians. All risk the vulnerability of sharing their faith and fears with others. It's so much simpler to isolate and separate oneself from what is happening in the outside world.

But in the midst of our doubts, we are called to reach out to one another. Such a stance moves us beyond survival or mere self-fulfillment. Knowing that another person in Christ accepts and values us as we are encourages us to continue reaching out to others. And encouragement is what each of us knows we desperately need.

Ministry is not primarily individual acts of service, but experience of God's gift of grace to the community of faith. It is the gift of God to the whole people of God. And that means accountability.

Someone has said we are not here to see through one another, but to see each other through. The tie is blessed that binds us to one another. What are some ways in which a congregation nurtures accountability?

**1. Prayer**
In worship, our prayers of confession and forgiveness bring us before God and one another. The presence of God's grace is what sustains us in all our other relationships of accountability.

**2. Personal Encouragement**
In Bible study and prayer groups, individual members encourage one another to be bearers of the Word in the world of beauty parlors, garages, and planning offices. They learn to be effective listeners and care givers for one another.

### 3. Commissioning Services
Some congregations have commissioning services in which all the people engaged in a particular occupation (teaching, health care, office management) are recognized on a Sunday morning as the congregation's ministers to that field of work. Those people meet together, usually once a week for a few weeks, to discuss their line of work in terms of its faith implications and opportunities. They may raise up particular issues deserving of concerted action or concern on the part of the Christian community and develop action plans for involving themselves or the congregation in the issue. Such a commissioning service itself is a sort of accountability exercise. It is a way of saying, "You are our representatives in this area, and we expect you to minister faithfully in it."

### 4. Special Training
Training courses in areas such as listening, communication, and caring ministry become much more important and valuable to the one who bears responsibility for being the peacemaker, reconciler, or healer in the office place.

### Opportunity and Challenge

To have mutual accountability, a congregation needs to provide opportunity for sharing one's faith and fears. In small groups with Bible study and prayer, we can risk our vulnerability. Such groups need not be formally structured but could be the linking of three neighbor women meeting together weekly, two nurses in a local hospital having an occasional bag-lunch, or a half-dozen men breakfasting together in a diner. The agenda is no more and no less: How *in the world* are you doing? How is God working in your life? The results: encouragement, support, and accountability. Such actions build up the body of Christ.

In all our encounters with one another, intensive listening is absolutely essential. To listen with the whole self is to develop a sensitivity for what is left unsaid. Empathy is what is needed. We can then ask deeper questions so that the other can perhaps see the larger implications of what she is doing in the world. By not giving answers or solutions, we can assist the other to see alternatives and consequences of possible choices. And each of us is to be open to the risk of being accountable to the other.

Accountability includes both acceptance and challenge. The key is to respond with both, whether the other person is rejoicing or suffering. Such actions are what interdependence and mutuality of ministry are all about. By really listening and taking mutual expectations seriously, we will be able to move beyond the first stages of mere common complaint and surface support. We will be so certain of one another's deep acceptance that we will be able to risk becoming change agents for justice and bridge builders for reconciliation.

## Commentary

### by John Graff, a Virginia attorney

What if my congregation were to say to me . . . ?

"John, you are one of our representatives to the legal system. We expect you to use your talents and learning as a lawyer not just to do good legal work for your clients (though that is part of what it means to minister), but to work as a little Christ within the legal system to make sure it, in fact, produces justice for everyone.

"We would like you to report to us occasionally on how you see it going. Tell us what you are doing to improve the system. Tell us where the problems are so that as citizens we can act intelligently, through voting or advocacy, to make the changes to that system that are necessary.

"How do you, John, as the professional, see your faith bearing on such issues as capital punishment, court reform, or whatever?

"And then we, in turn, want to be accountable and responsible to you for support and encouragement. We will bear you up when you are beaten down. We will offer our advice and our prayers when you need wisdom.

"We will make it our business to know what you are doing and what we can do to help you with that ministry."

This is not the church judging how I practice law. That is the responsibility of the law schools and bar committees. It is the body of Christ, of which I am a part, recognizing my work for what it is. It is the body asking me to account for that work in terms of my calling as a Christian. It is the body offering to help equip me out of its understanding and experiences and to support me in my ministry.

There is risk in this. I might be found wanting in faithfulness. The congregation may suggest places where what our faith seems to require is at odds with what my profession may demand of me. The congregation may be less than wise in how it assesses my ministry or less than loving in how it perceives the difficulty of the choices I face.

Surely those risks are not such as to justify letting either me or the congregation off the hook. The call is to faithful ministry within the body. How can the body function if it does not know what the members are doing? How can the individual members serve effectively without the support and cooperation of the body?

The response to the suggestion of risk is that faith and ministry are inherently risky. We are not insulated from that. In fact, we are called to pick up even the cross if need be.

But is there not less risk of the community being destructive than of my failing on my own? Is it not more likely that I will be strengthened and sustained by the body of Christ striving to support me than that I will succeed on my own in being strong and faithful?

The surprise is that the idea of accountability in and to the congregation should be considered dangerous. We should have been much more intentional about it long ago.

The mission field today is not primarily some distant, unchurched land. It is main street and down the country lane. The missionaries to this mission field are people of faith who are also plumbers, nurses, farmers, and clerks.

The church needs to provide them with the same sort of training and support that goes into equipping people for mission work to other cultures. And it should expect and receive the same kind of accountability for what is going on out in the mission field.[1]

1.  Think of the ways your congregation nurtures accountability.

2.  Are there further ways to do so? How could Graff's ideas work in your congregation?

3.  What's risky in having conversations about each other's accountability? Is the risk worth it? Why?

# PART 4

# How in the world is the Church?

To take the temperature of the church, to say how it is doing in today's world, is really almost impossible. The church's many different manifestations deter us, but that's only one obstacle; we have difficulty getting a true perspective on the very times in which we live.

Having said that, we ask: How vital is the church as we approach the end of the millennium? Declining membership, especially among the younger generation, marks most denominations. A preoccupation with survival seems dominant.

So how is the church to go about its work? The final four chapters elaborate on each of the following themes of the church in mission in the world.

First, the congregation sets the climate for ministry and mission by creating a trustworthy climate. Such a climate takes seriously the people who are the actors in this real-life drama of God and God's people, even when the plot is full of danger.

Second, the congregation sees itself not as a passive group staying within a building, but as part of the great procession of Christians of all times and places who have come together to worship and then go out to serve in the world.

Third, the congregation supports its people in connecting faith and daily life. By doing theology in the language of the people, we can listen, probe, support, and together respond to the call to discipleship. A congregation that has found ways to share struggles and connect with one another and God experiences renewal and new direction.

Finally, the congregation takes upon itself the adventure of risk, of putting everything on the line for Christ's sake. We all hunger for challenge.

CHAPTER 11

# Setting the Stage

Long before the play happens, even before the actors are certain of all
their lines, the director and the set designer are consulting with each
other about the setting of the stage. Their questions: What will be the
overall climate of this production? What is the mood to be established?
What atmosphere will permeate the action so fully that most of the audience will not really notice how deeply the shapes, colors, and lighting
have influenced them?

Every congregation has a stage setting. Certain elements such as
location and style of building already convey much to both the members
and everyone else. But it is the intangible elements that are crucial for
setting the climate and atmosphere of the congregation. These elements
precede as well as permeate the specific actions that take place within the
church. The climate is perceived more through attitudes and understand-
ings than through particular actions. So the question becomes: What
attitudes about ministry and mission pervade the congregation? Consider the following situations:

- Let the pastor do it. After all, the pastor is paid to witness, to call on
  the sick, to work in the community.
- I feel guilty. I declined to be nominated for the church council
  because my work on the town school board is pretty demanding
  right now.
- Peg just died and she was our closest neighbor. I know she was
  having a rough time. Her husband was out of work. I wonder if the
  church did anything; I don't think the pastor came out to see her.
- I don't know if we should go ahead. Before we as the church council

talk about this new idea of members working on this need within the
community, we must see that the church building is in good shape.

• I'm a new member and feel God's call. I am praying to find what
  that means and going to a class at church to learn more.

• I feel overwhelmed. Since nobody around the church seems to want
  to do anything, I as the pastor am stuck with doing it all.

• We've been lifelong members of this church. What were *they* thinking of when *they* started a food pantry in *our* church?

• As pastor, I'm really proud of *my* church.

• This church is really growing. I think it's because people want a
  church that is adventurous and challenging as well as loving and
  accepting.

**Reflection**

Look again at the above situations.

1.  Which of them, either stated or implied, ring true about attitudes
    within your congregation?
2.  Which of them would you want to be true of your congregation?
3.  How is a climate formed, and how is it changed?
4.  How could a healthy, hospitable climate be encouraged?

# Images of the Church

How do you see the church and particularly your congregation or parish?
How does it see itself?

All of us see the world around us in images and word pictures. A
church at worship, for example, can be seen as rows of faceless people,
impersonal and distant. Members can be perceived as gears in a machine
or as plants that need growth and nurture. Often such images are implicit
rather than explicit, but no one doubts that they do make a difference in
how we see one another and how we set the stage.

Of the following images—biblical, theological, and practical—
which is operative for you about your congregation? What other images
can you see?

**The People of God**

This image is deeply rooted in the biblical revelation; you are my people, God says over and over in the Old Testament. And the church is the new people of God, baptized by God's grace. First Peter 2:9-10 says: "You are a chosen race, a royal priesthood, a holy nation, God's own people .... Once you were not a people, but now you are God's people."

This meaning has been recovered in our day, especially since Vatican II, for it was the controlling theme in *Lumen Gentium.* To be called the people of God does not convey special privileges, but rather special responsibility. The people of God are set apart, not in isolation but called to be disciples and ambassadors, to be the people of God in the world. When we leave our worship, we are God's people carrying that name and that message.

**A Caring Fellowship**

Luther once called the congregation a fellowship of mutual conversation and consolation. There are ways for that to happen, through shepherding programs, prayer circles, and Bible study groups to support, comfort, encourage, and challenge one another as we are in a caring fellowship in Christ. The people care for one another and for those around them.

**The Theater of God's Activity**

In his book *Purity of Heart*, Sören Kierkegaard compares our relationships within the church with the roles in the theater.[1] In the theater the prompter is the one who remains hidden, whispering the words the actor needs to speak; the audience passively observes the action and assumes all the important action is manifested through the role of the actor. It is not accurate, says Kierkegaard (even though it is how we usually distribute the roles), to see God as the prompter who gives the words to the pastor as the actor on stage who assumes the imparted message to be the main action, and to see the congregation as the passive audience. It would be more correct to visualize all members of the congregation as the main actors on the stage of life in the drama of service, the pastor as the prompter, and God as the role of audience encouraging all the players, on and off stage.

## The Company of the Committed

Elton Trueblood has made this image alive for all of us in his excellent book titled *The Company of the Committed.*2  The church building is the headquarters of the committed; the field is the world. This image can be expressed even more dramatically.  The church is like a company of paratroopers who are trained on Sunday, then on Monday morning they are "dropped"—to land in various places across the community. Such a sense of urgency would really give us pause as we think about being mobilized and equipped for our daily lives to infiltrate, not with weapons of death but with words and deeds of life. The congregation is the place to mobilize and equip each of us for the tasks of ministry in the world of our daily lives.

## An Irrigation Ditch

This rather bold image of the church as an irrigation ditch emphasizes that the purpose of the church is to spread the living water through the thirsty and arid world around us. The intent is a variation of the image of the church as the community in which hungry people are always telling other hungry people where to find food. It is exciting to see the mission of the congregation as giving cups of cold water and sharing fresh bread so that people are nourished. Whether viewed as a place where fresh bread and cold water are provided or as a channel through which water is dispersed, the church refreshes and renews us.

## A Cloud of Witnesses

The source of this image is the familiar Hebrews 12:1: "Therefore, since we are surrounded by so great a cloud of witnesses, let us also lay aside every weight, and sin that clings so closely, and let us run with perseverance the race that is set before us."

A church in the Midwest has inscribed this passage near the ceiling in its circular worship sanctuary. Following the passage, encircling the sanctuary, are written the names of Adam, Eve, Abel, Noah, Sarah, other Old Testament figures, then Mary and the New Testament disciples, early Christian believers, through the Reformers, and more recent people of faith up to Dietrich Bonhoeffer. The space left in the circle at the end affirms that the journey of the Christian faith continues with us called to add each others' names for this time and place.

**The Body of Christ**

Saint Paul gives us this great crescendo image: "Now you are the body of Christ and individually members of it" (1 Cor. 12:27). He was writing not to an ideal church, but to Corinth—with its divisions and problems. Paul points out vividly that every member of the body is necessary for the body to function properly as an organic living body. When any part of the body does not function properly, the whole body is affected.

We are members, not in the sense of being dues-paying subscribers, but members in the sense of being arms and legs, knees and elbows, eyes and ears of the body of Christ. We are knit together, members of Christ and members of one another.

## Commentary

### by Gregory Pierce, a lay Catholic from Chicago

Let me offer you a model for the church that I have found to be very helpful to my fellow Catholics, as well as for people in other denominations. It is the model of the church as a campaign headquarters. In Chicago, where politics is so pervasive that it has become a spectator sport, it is very natural for us to think of everything in terms of politics. I am not talking here about "the church being more involved in politics." As a matter of fact, to the extent that good Catholics and good

Lutherans and good Christians are involved in government and politics, the church is already involved in politics. That's not the issue I'm talking about.

I'm talking about using the political reality of the campaign headquarters as a model of the church. What is a campaign headquarters? What happens at it? It is a place where people go to meet each other, to learn about candidates and issues, to pick up materials, to receive assignments—so that they can go out and wage a campaign. During the campaign, they return to the campaign headquarters to celebrate their victories, lick their wounds, pick up reinforcements and get ready to go back out to continue the campaign. If there is no campaign, the campaign headquarters looks—to paraphrase Cardinal Newman's famous quote about a church without laity—pretty silly.

If you look at the church—and specifically the local congregation—as a campaign headquarters, it raises three immediate questions:

1.   What is the campaign?
2.   Who are the campaign field workers?
3.   What is the job of the campaign headquarters workers?

The answer to the first question should be obvious. The campaign for all Christians of all denominations is the spreading of the Gospel, the good news, which we are not only to proclaim with our lips but to live "always and in all ways."

The campaign field workers are all baptized Christians. By the very act of being baptized, we all—laity and clergy, ordained or not—sign up for a lifetime stint as field workers for the campaign.

Who then are the campaign headquarters workers? They are those few—mostly clergy with an increasing number of laity, mostly paid with an increasing number of volunteers—whose job it is to be of service to the workers in the field. If the campaign headquarters is not efficiently and effectively useful to those workers in the field, then it is not doing its job. The criteria for judging the success or failure of the campaign headquarters workers is not whether they build a bigger or better campaign headquarters (and certainly not whether they get more and more people to volunteer to work at campaign headquarters), but rather how helpful they are in recognizing, supporting, and challenging the workers in the field.

If you can buy this model at least for a moment, then you will see that the church would have to operate much differently. What is needed is to look at every single activity of the Church and to ask whether it is truly aimed at helping the "worker within the field."[3]

1. What in this model of the church do you find significant? What is limiting?

2. If your congregation adopted this model, what changes would have to be made?

Paul Minear, in his classic, insightful book *Images of the Church in the New Testament,* shows that there are more than eighty (one hundred if the Greek words are counted separately) images.[4] This gallery of images is not for objective measurement but to awaken the imagination: salt of the earth, letter from Christ, vine and branches, fish and fishnet, light of the world, unleavened bread, table of the Lord, the new creation. Each conveys a sense of identity and mission. Neither salt nor vine nor table nor light exists for itself. The salt preserves and sometimes irritates; the light illuminates; the vine produces fruit. No one image is sufficient to communicate the whole activity of God and God's people.

Each of these images underlines that the church and each of our congregations exists not for itself, but on behalf of the world. We are called to be the salt of the earth, not the salt of the salt. The church is not an end in itself, but to be a faithful witness and presence of Christ in the

world around us. We are to be Christ's living body that moves from the
service of the Word to service in the world.

### Reflection

1.  Let your mind wander to various memories of the church as you
    have experienced it. Who is there? What is going on? What images
    do you see?
2.  Consider the faith community that you know best now. What image
    would you give it?
3.  How do other members view it? Play with these images.
4.  What image would people walking (or driving) around your neigh-
    borhood use to identify this congregation?
5.  What images might be helpful for this congregation to become more
    clear about its identity?
6.  How do these images help people see their mission in the world?

## The Relationship of the Church and the World

Images of the church thus set the stage for our ministry and mission, but
our framework for understanding the church in relationship to the world
is also pivotal for the climate of the congregation.

Is the church a sacred little island in the middle of a secular and
pagan world? Are we as church members like commuters shuttling back
and forth between church and world with limited commitments to both?
Is the church primarily the comfort station to heal the wounds we receive
out in the world?

H. Richard Niebuhr, in his classic book *Christ and Culture*, gives
five typical answers to the enduring problem. He uses "Christ" here to
mean Jesus Christ and all who believe in and follow Christ, and "culture"
as the total process of human activity, its language, achievements, values,
structures, and social organization. The five types of relationships are as
follows:

1. Christ *against* culture. Whatever the customs of the society in
which Christians live, and whatever the human achievements it conserves,

Christ is opposed to them, so Christians have an either/or decision to make.

2. The Christ *of* culture. There is fundamental agreement that Jesus' life and teachings are regarded as the greatest human achievement. Christians regard Christ as one good among many good things.

3. Christ *above* culture. Christ is the fulfillment of culture and re-storer of the institutions of true society. Christ enters into life from above with gifts for human aspiration.

4. Christ and culture in *paradox*. Christians throughout life face a tension. They are citizens of two worlds. All of culture, including human-kind, is broken and under God's judgment. God's love brings faith, hope, and love.

5. Christ the *transformer* of culture. The fallenness of humankind needs to be recognized, yet this does not call for separation from the world but for the task of conversion, changing the culture.[5]

Any or all of these types of answers to the question of the relation-ship between Christ and culture may be found in one congregation. Even though we may not discuss the issues this way, the relationship between Christ and culture may be the issue behind the issues over which we disagree. Compounding the problem is the fact that the church is both "Christ" (meaning part of the body of Christ) and also a human institu-tion—a part of "culture" that continually needs to be redeemed and transformed.

God "so loved the world," both its people and the creation. God has called us to live in "holy worldliness."[6] And the emphasis is both on holiness and worldliness. Why? Because our task is to work to extend Christ's reign, which encompasses ground much broader than "the church."

The archbishop of Canterbury, George Carey, puts the matter directly:

I want to challenge a theology and a history which automatically assumes that the center of Christianity is the Church rather than the world. We have grown up with a "geocentric" vision that what we do as Christians in the church is more significant in our discipleship than what we do in our daily work as executives, university profes-sors, engineers, lawyers, and so on. A Copernican vision is required of us to see at the center of God's mission not the splendid work of church but the equally splendid life wilderness of the world. . . . At the heart of this is the fact that Christ came into His world and sent his disciples into this world. Christ came to bring us a Kingdom not a Church.[7]

### Reflection and Discussion

1.  Which of Niebuhr's five types reflect your understanding of the relationship of Christ and culture?
2.  Has that varied in different periods of your life?
3.  Think of people or views in your congregation that reflect some of the other types.
4.  How do these views affect the way we understand the church's mission?
5.  How can we seek to understand where each other is coming from?
6.  What challenge do you see in Archbishop Carey's words?

## Setting the Stage for Action

To focus on the congregation's and the member's mission in the world, we need to explore the various views people have of the relationship between Christ and culture. We can imagine and play with possible images of the church, and expand these through biblical exploration.

We can also help set the stage for action. The marquee out front does not promise only one star: the pastor (even though some people pick a church by who's preaching this Sunday). The marquee reads: "Now playing: God and God's people." We, directors, stage hands, actors, can all help set the stage of God's drama.

1. Prepare an environment of trust and acceptance. Because God has accepted each person in unconditional love, we accept one another.

2. Check the acoustics. Listen, really listen to one another. Make sure all can hear and that all have a speaking role.

3. Make sure all can enter. Who knows where the stage door is? Can people in the community find the main entrance? Is this place

accessible for all?  Are certain seats reserved?  Does class or race still determine box seating or upper balcony?

4.  Let people know they can come as they are. Many people stay away from a faith community because they think they don't have a presentable outward appearance. We are invited to bring all our pain, our problems, and to take off our masks. God chooses not to be critic, but playwright; not villain, but lover.

5.  This drama is promised a long run. God is faithful and will not forsake God's people. We can trust that promise. We need to set a stage that is open and inclusive and faithful. We need a trustworthy space for people to be different together, so we don't step on one another's toes, interrupt one another's lines, but rather play off of one another, encouraging one another for the long run.

6.  Help people feel a sense of call. Everyone receives a call-back in this drama because all people are necessary to fill an infinite number of roles. There are no small parts, no useless gifts. Each individual is called to develop his or her particular gifts to their full potential for an ensemble that brings a theater to life.

7.  Let the music rise and the action excite people. We can cherish past plays, but this drama is a live performance. With the stage set, we are comfortably ready to play our part, to be challenged—and to go forth into the aisles and out onto the avenue for improvisational street theater.

The stage is set. Let the drama proceed!

## CHAPTER 12

# *Worshipping in the Great Procession*

Last Sunday, about 40 percent of all Americans attended worship.

Imagine, will you, this huge throng as one long procession.

There would be all ages—from infants carried in a parent's arms to the hobbling aged. People of color, people from all economic backgrounds, some dignified, others casual all would be moving to houses of worship.

And what would this diverse crowd have in common? Certainly not much on the surface of things. But what we share is that this is the people of God.

The image of the people of God is at the center of both the Hebrew Scriptures and the New Testament. God calls and chooses a people not because they are good, not because they have attained holiness, and not because they never go astray. In fact, the Scriptures speak of the journeying of a people who again and again lose their way and again and again are called back.

One picture of the church, then, and of your congregation and mine, as Celia Hahn suggests, is "a company of needy people on pilgrimage."[1] After all, the early followers of Christ were called the people of the Way (Acts 9:2).

First impressions of that great procession would be that many of the participants are decent looking, marching at a steady pace. But look more closely. Certainly some are walking with confidence, a few are running enthusiastically, but others are crawling, and a number are being supported and even carried.

As all of us come to worship, we come with the joys and struggles of the past week. We bring with us, like it or not, burdens that haunt us, anxieties that trouble us, excitements that distract us. We come with all the ambiguity of being saints, already incorporated through baptism into the people of God, and we come as sinners in deep need of confession and forgiveness. We have come to bring all of ourselves before God to respond to the love that was shown in calling us, of all people, to be God's people. We have come to worship.

On Palm Sunday each year, Nelvin's congregation has a procession of all the worshippers. We begin outdoors and then proceed down the long aisle to receive our palms at the altar. The hymn is usually "All Glory, Laud, and Honor," and we sing lustily. At the same time, however, as this praise is being offered, we are uncomfortably aware that this is the Sunday of the Passion. Later in the week, we too will crucify Christ once again. And finally, we remember that this worship service, as all Christian worship, is a little Easter, a concrete action and response to celebrate the resurrection of Christ.

So there we all are in that procession each time we worship: a praising people, a crucifying people, a resurrected people. We are weak and fragile, limping along, and at the same time, strengthened and nourished.

## The Gathered and the Scattered

In worship we are the gathered people of God. We come together as the community of faith, as the assembled body of believers, as the corporate members of Christ's body. We are, in short, a congregation, which means, literally, being collected into a flock.

This image, this understanding of the church as the gathered people, is the predominant image when we speak of the church. We go to church, we say; we do things for the church. To see the church as the assembled people of God baptized in Christ's name is certainly accurate. At the same time, if the question is asked: "Where is the church at eleven o'clock on Monday morning?" the answer is, "The church is where each of us is, in our homes, offices, factories, schoolrooms, farms, and all other places; that is where the members of the body of Christ, the church, are."

And that dimension of the church is often called the scattered church. Interestingly, that very term, *scattered,* betrays a doubleness that is also expressed in our earlier image of the great procession on the way to worship. On the one hand, the connotations of *scattered* move toward *dispersed, diffused,* even *dissipated, diminished, adrift.* But on the other hand, the meanings of *scattered* evoke the characteristics of seeds ripe for growth: *widespread, disseminated, broadcast, planted* in many different, particular places.

When we think of worship, we remember that we are not only a *gathered* people but also a *scattered* people. We have come from a multitude of places and situations, and next week we will again face unexpected hills and valleys. And when we move out of the church building, each of us is seeking to make connections between the symbols of faith and the stuff of ordinary life.

All of us face many questions and dilemmas each week. But God is not out for the perfection we want. In the midst of the ups and downs of our daily lives, God is looking for the trust, the faith, the love, the picking up of pieces, the coming back. This flip-flop, rollercoaster-of-life experience is what we bring with us as we journey to worship.


**Reflection**

As you gather for worship, consider where you have been all week.

1.   What does forgiveness mean in those settings?
2.   What are the challenges I bring to this gathered assembly?
3.   Where have other people been since we last saw one another?
4.   How does my baptism relate to my week's work?
5.   How does the Lord's Supper connect with the meals I ate this week?

As you go forth—back home, back to work—ask yourself these same five questions.


# What Worship Is About

Within this "journey" image are several very important questions for congregations to ask: What are the needs of the worshippers as they come together? What are their expectations? Where have they been? Where are they going? These concrete questions will help to connect worship and the daily lives of Christians.

Such an approach is not to be written off as being selfishly centered on our needs; it is not viewing worship only as a means to an end. To praise God, to glorify Christ's name, to ask for the guidance of the Holy Spirit, to confess our sins, and to be absolved *are* what Christians need.

Without thanksgiving to God, forgiveness in Christ, and the presence of the Holy Spirit, our lives are not meaningful. To worship means to bring the whole self before God. We offer up our total lives before God's presence. In the experiences of worship we leave nothing unopened to God, and the various acts of worship help us to do exactly that.

Both worship leaders and participants too frequently assume that worship pertains only to the spiritual, the devotional, as Mark Gibbs aptly termed it, "the congregation as a little local holy huddle."[2] Then the gap between Sunday and Monday becomes impossible to bridge. To shut out our daily joys and tensions is not what worship is all about. Rather, worship is the offering of our whole lives as a testimony of God's love for us and for all of creation. The experience of worship helps us to be sustained and strengthened with the knowledge and the trust that God is with us not only here in worship, but also in the crisis and in the ordinary round of next week's activities. Each element of worship can equip and support us for the ongoing journey.

## Go To and From and Through

How then does worship equip and support this diverse company of pilgrims for the journey?

One way of beginning to answer that huge question is to understand the church as a place to go to, a place to go from, and a place to go through. Of course, the church is not first of all a place; it is a people. Yet these three dimensions may help us see how worship as the central act of the Christian faith equips and supports us for the ongoing journey.

### The Church: A Place to Go To

Psalms 8 and 24 are usually interpreted as songs of praise chanted as the worshippers ascended to the entrance of the temple:

O Lord, our Sovereign,
> how majestic is your name in all the earth! (Ps. 8:1).

The earth is the Lord's and all that is in it,
> the world, and those who live in it (Ps. 24:1).

The rising crescendo of voices joins together in praise and thanksgiving as they come to the place of worship.

One dimension of worship of the people of God is to honor, to reverence, to be aware of the worth of God, as indicated in the root meaning of the word *worship*. The people of God are already redeemed; they are the beneficiaries of God's love. What is there to do but to say and to sing praise to the holy name of God? What is there to do but to pray, "Lord, have mercy"?

The mighty acts of God are all around us; Christ has saved us; in the past, present, and future, the Holy Spirit continues to be with us. The response is confession and praise, and the church gathered in worship is the place to go to as we join in giving thanks to God and being nourished by the Word and the sacraments.

## The Church: A Place to Go From

Ephesians 4 speaks clearly and directly: God gives gifts to apostles, prophets, evangelists, pastors, and teachers. For what purpose? To equip the saints for the work of ministry.

As emphasized in this understanding, the purpose of the church is to teach and to train. The worship service is part of the mobilizing of the company of Christians and the launching area for facing the struggles of the coming week. The teaching of the Word, the sharing of the Eucharist, and the participation in baptism and all else are part of the equipping to be the church in the world, to be the body of Christ.

The gathered church at worship is therefore the place to go from as we attempt to live faithfully in witness and service in the arenas of daily life.

## The Church: A Place to Go Through

Hebrews 11 and 12 again give us direction for this understanding of the people of God. A host of pilgrims is ahead of us: By faith Abraham and Sarah and Isaac and Jacob and Moses and "time would fail me to tell of. . . ." The opening of the twelfth chapter places each of us within that procession: "Therefore, since we are surrounded by so great a cloud of witnesses, let us also lay aside every weight, and the sin that clings so closely, and let us run with perseverance the race that is set before us."

This is the people of God on the move, on the journey. The procession *is* the church. Around us and before us and with us, the faithful community is formed by the power of the Spirit. The pilgrims move to the places of worship to praise, and we depart from there having been equipped. In addition, we have been strengthened and nourished and freed to be once again the people of God.

A people coming to worship are in need, in need of confession, in need of being forgiven, in need of praise and thanksgiving, in need of encouragement and support. Therefore, supplication, petition, and intercession permeate worship. Having been nourished by the Word, by the sacraments, and by the fellowship of the believing community, we are inspired to continue.

Worship then is a kind of oasis, a temporary stopping point to be refreshed. The oasis is not the primary goal of the journey; it is the means to continue the ongoing movement. The sick are given new life, the grieving are assured consolation, and all are renewed to continue the caring and serving that God uses as the means to make Christ's love real.

In worship we hear the call to come, to come to the Lord's house to praise the Lord's name, to come apart to rest awhile, to come to the altar and to the table. But at the same time, in worship, we hear the call to go, to "go into all the world."

In such coming and going, the congregation at worship equips and supports its members in their daily journeys.

## Worship as Work of the People of God

What are some particular areas that worship leaders and worship committees may review to determine how worship may more fully affirm,
equip, and support the members of the congregation in their daily lives?

- Do members of the congregation take leadership roles within the
  worship service?  If so, are they trained?  Is their selection carefully
  done, based on their gifts and their representation of the congregation?
- Does the bulletin include a listing of the various ministries that
  members are rendering within the worship service?  Could your
  bulletin use this kind of designation?
      The Ministers of Saint Luke:  All the Members
      The Pastor of Saint Luke:  Rev. Janet Heffner
- Do the hymns carry out the theme of the worship as well as give
  guidance to the members in their daily lives?
- Are the prayers concrete and specific?  Do they include not only
  prayers for the suffering of the sick and grieving, but also thanksgiving for the joys within the congregation and in the world?
- What elements and approaches in sermons help members to see
  connections between faith and daily life?
- What are we giving to the Lord in our offering?
- Why is silence important within the worship service?

Some broader areas for discussion:

- Explore the term *liturgy* as "the work of the people."  What does
  such an understanding imply?  Uses?  Possible abuses?
- How important is the sacrament of baptism in the worship of the
  congregation?  In what ways may baptism be a time for affirming all
  members in their ministry?
- In what ways may Holy Communion be celebrated not only as a
  feast for God's people, but also as a daily nourishment for our life in
  the world?
- Does the worship involve our whole beings:  the heart, the mind, the
  soul, the body, the emotions, the senses?

The church indeed is a place to go to and from, a place to go through, a place to go into and then out of.

The word *service* itself carries such meanings. The worship service is a ritualistic action, the primary purpose of which is to serve God, and then, in response, we are to serve others. Both at the opening and at the closing of worship, it is appropriate to say: Let the service begin!

## CHAPTER 13

# Connecting the People

Connecting is what our lives are about. We begin our lives connected to our parents and connected to God in baptism. We are all members of a larger family of some kind as well as members of a community. No matter what our gender, race, class, or role, we are connected to one another in our common humanity, even though we frequently reject or deny these connections. In the last several decades, we have recognized our global connectedness not only politically and economically, but also in our direct awareness of world hunger and international terror. We are linked to one another, whether we like it or not, whether we want to be or not.

But some connections are unhealthy. When we are enmeshed, we feel trapped. Oppression and invasion are unjust connections, whether due to individual people or nations. Connections are helpful only if who or what is being linked provides for the growth of each party involved.

Many of the struggles and tensions in our lives are rooted in a lack of connection. Family conflict, problems where we work, violence within our neighborhoods and the country, international misunderstandings— all of these flow from our inability and unwillingness to relate fully and deeply to one another. Sin and evil have sometimes been described as the gap, the dysfunction between God and human beings. We separate and isolate and take apart and pull asunder that which is intended to be together. Sometimes we feel disjointed, disconnected inside. The parts of our life fall apart; we see only the pieces, the fragments.

A very fundamental question with which each of us struggles is this: How is my Christian faith connected with the challenges, the joys, and all the happenings in my daily life? How do the realities of daily living (stress, competition, success, compromise, conflict) relate to the realities of faith (prayer, the presence of God)? How do I attempt to put my life together?

This chapter invites the reader to recognize the connections already present in one's life, provides some insights on how to deal with the gaps—the lack of connection—and discusses ways to be supported and equipped to grow spiritually within our faith communities and amid the hustle and bustle of our daily lives.

## Reflection

1.  Are there parts of your life that feel disconnected? Take some time to probe the issues and relationships that contribute to the disconnection.
2.  What connections—people in your family and congregation—strengthen you?
3.  What national or global disconnections or conflicts trouble you? What at base is the problem?

# Connecting with God

In a real sense, we as human beings cannot and need not do the connecting. We cannot do the connecting because our deceitfulness distorts our perception of and willingness to live our commitment connected to Christ. We need not do the connecting because God has already connected everything; the creation, even with its brokenness, is a universe, a oneness. Christ's coming into our human life, by dying and rising victoriously, reunited us and bridged the gap and connects us eternally.

# Easter Life Is Connected

*Excerpt from an Easter sermon by James Wolford*

If we affirm that there was a risen Christ, we must take seriously what the risen Christ said about us. He said the power of God will appear in us. "You will," he said, "be clothed with power from on high." He said that when we proclaim repentance and offer forgiveness, we are the voice of God speaking. We cannot affirm the risen Christ and at the same time deny the infinite depth and importance of our lives.

Let's say that tomorrow you pray for world peace. Or you may let a car stuck at a yield sign move into line ahead of you. Maybe you will forgive the person who forgot to memo you about the change in a meeting date. You may even take the unusual step for a reserved Christian of talking about God. Some people see nothing terribly significant about any of those. Maybe you don't either. Happenstance, whim, no big deal. The risen Christ, however, sees eternal significance. In the world of the Spirit, in the depths below the surface, all life is connected. Just as a touch at any point on a spider web sets the whole thing trembling, so each act, good or bad, sets the universe trembling. There are no unimportant acts any more than there is a heaven empty of God. Just because we don't see it doesn't mean it isn't there.[1]

1. Do you perceive all of life to be connected? Why?

2. Trace one seemingly insignificant act and its consequences.

The talk of the relationship between our Christian faith and daily living may also be misleading. It assumes that there are two separate worlds: faith and daily life. It acts as it there were two entities—God and world—that depend on us to put the two together. But we do not have two separate lives—that is, a spiritual life and the remaining part of life. In fact, our faith commitment is frequently so entangled in mundane affairs that we do not know where the one begins and the other ends. If a baby is baptized in the family, that may involve arranging flight schedules for grandparents and preparing food for the big family gathering. Is it possible to sort out which of these actions are mundane?

Some particular words are important about our faith and daily life: *relate, link, intersect;* others could be added: *bridge, meet, integrate.* What they all imply is a putting together, a unifying of our faith and our action, our commitment and our practice. They all imply an *and*—that little word that is one of the most important we hear and use. The Swiss theologian Karl Barth once said: "'And' is one of the most interesting and difficult words in language: heaven and earth, male and female, God and man."[2] We would add faith *and* daily life.

## Connecting with the Church

The usual way of getting at the lack of connectedness between our faith and our living goes something like this: (1) Christians in their daily lives have struggles and problems. (2) The church is the place that has the answers to these problems. (3) Christians take these answers and apply them to the problems and issues they face.

There are several serious flaws in this approach. An understanding of the church as the place for answers only and not for questions discourages Christians from admitting and discussing their struggles. One occasionally hears: Well, almost everyone else in my congregation has his or her act together, and I'm the only one still struggling. Feeling that way, we hesitate to ask the sticky questions out loud for fear of embarrassment; we're afraid to reveal how weak our faith is amid all these churchy people. By not sharing our worries and our doubts, we deprive one another of the encouragement each of us needs. The congregation is to be a safe place to reflect on one's fears and one's faith.

The role of church leaders is distorted if it is assumed that the church has or should have all the answers. Let's put it bluntly: Pastors are people too! Any pastor or other church leader will confess that he or she struggles, experiences tensions with families or friends, and has to decide how to respond to what is happening in the community. They, like all of us, are attempting to relate faith and life. And it's usually no easier for them to do that than it is for anyone else. But by identifying with one another, pastors and laity may mutually support one another.

The most fundamental error in this description is that it ignores the fact that God is at work among us at all times and at all places. That is true not only in worship and at our times of prayer, as essential as they are. Rather, God is at work in the world around us, in our places of work, at our breakfast tables with their shared joys and quarrels, in our decisions on how to care for the Earth, in our political processes—and all else. Again, we don't have to "haul God in," for Christ's redemptive power and Holy Spirit's guiding love is around us and within us. By assuming that Christians are not already making some of the connections between faith and life, we neither affirm their faith nor do we avail ourselves of listening to and responding to these stories of deep and probing faith right among us.

## Reflection

Take one situation in your current daily life. Probe that situation—the dilemmas, challenges, and possibilities.

1. What's going on?
2. How may God be working in the situation?
3. What connections is God making?

Discussing this with a trusted friend may help in the discernment process.

## Connecting Ministry and Daily Life

Within the last few decades, the term *ministry* has been expanded to include the work of the people of God. The *laos*, the people of God, of
course, have been *doing* ministry all along, even when it was not so
named. Typical of such description is that found in the World Council of
Churches' document *Baptism, Eucharist and Ministry* (1982): "The
word *ministry* in its broadest sense denotes the service to which the
whole people of God is called, whether as individuals, as a local community, or as the universal Church." *Minister* is from the Latin *ministro*
which means to serve, to attend, to wait on. A minister is one who serves.
To be a minister is to be "the lesser one," the opposite of master, "the
greater one."

The biblical witness is rooted in such an understanding. Paul de-
clared that Tychicus was "a faithful minister in the Lord" (Eph. 6:21) and
that Epaphras was "a faithful minister of Christ" (Col. 1:7). What does
this mean? Simply that these people were good servants, faithful in all
their relationships.

The statement that every Christian is called to minister for the sake
of Christ is not affirmed in order to achieve a certain status or to dilute
the meaning of ordained ministry of Word and Sacrament. Rather, such
an understanding is both an affirmation of what already is and also a
challenge to each member of the body of Christ. The whole ministry is
given to the whole church for the whole world. Yet certain distortions
creep into our use of the word. Pastors as well as others may speak of *the*
ministry ("When I entered the ministry . . ."). Other distortions occur:
"holy ministry" (as if some ministry were unholy or less holy), "public
ministry" (as if some ministry were private), or "full-time ministry" (as if
some Christians were in part-time service to Christ). Such phrases affirm
neither the calling of all Christians in their baptism nor the mutuality and
interdependence of the whole people of God.

Our words, as we know, are usually a reflection of what we are
thinking. And since our words about laity have been shifting over the last
two decades or so, perhaps our thinking about the people of God is also
undergoing some change.

**Lay Ministry**

Up to the 1960s the term of choice was *lay ministry*. That included everything: people—members of church staffs who were laity—as well as acts of service, such as teaching Sunday church school or visiting the sick and delivering meals to the elderly.

Today the term *lay ministry* has been pretty well abandoned by most groups. Not only did the adjective *lay* imply "amateur" or "secondary" in contrast to ordained ministry, but also the term was primarily confined to church or religious activities. In addition the term sounds too "churchy." More crucially, the words *lay ministry* are not usually helpful because they will usually not attract the very people one wants to attract: those who are wrestling with complex and sensitive issues in their personal and professional lives but often do not find the institutional church addressing such matters.

**Ministry of the Laity**

The most common term in the seventies and early eighties was *ministry of the laity*. This phrase placed ministry in the primary position and reflected the understanding that all Christians are in ministry. But at the same time, it immediately sets up a dichotomy: ministry of the laity and ministry of the clergy.

When the terms *lay ministry* or *ministry of the laity* were central, the discussion would inevitably begin and often end with the distinction between clergy and laity. Granted, distinctiveness is important. But it must be said loudly and clearly that while many clergy and theologians are seemingly obsessed with spelling out carefully all the differences between clergy and laity, the vast majority of the people of God are not very interested in that question. To sort out all the various forms of ministry is important for internal order and clarity. But the issues involved are not a burning matter for most people in the pews.

Most of the people of God are not first of all concerned about the ministries of those who have church careers or even how much more can be done for the church. The reality of the people of God is filled with the business of getting and keeping a job, serving meals to the family, running computer programs, changing diapers, fixing leaky pipes, and helping our children move toward maturity. In many countries of the world, it takes everything to keep just body and soul together. After a long day in front of the glare of a word processor or of pumping gas, how important is the distinction of ministries of the laity in relation to the ordained? The huge and overwhelming questions are these: Why is all of this happening to me? How is what I do connected to my Christian faith? Where is God in all this? Where do I look for support for what I face? What does it mean for me to serve God and my neighbor? How is my life a response to God working in me?

### Ministry in Daily Life

*Ministry in daily life,* the more recent term used in several church circles, reflects such a concreteness and specificity. This term does not set up a duality between ministry of the laity and ministry of the clergy, but affirms that all Christians, including clergy, have a ministry in daily life. The calling of the ordained is neither denied nor minimized; it simply is not central. The arenas of occupation and family, of church and outreach, of community and leisure—in all such places and relationships, our ministry takes place.

The small word *in*—ministry in daily life—underlines not only the fact that the people of God are always in the world, but also that the particular calling of the people of God is to be the salt and leaven in where they already are. Christians are to live deeply in the world.

For the world is not over there; it is here all around us.

And ministry is not over there; it is where we already are.

Ministry in the world, in daily life—that connection is the challenge and adventure for every one of us!

## Called to Connect

If one begins with the understanding that the church is Christ's servants in the world, what might the congregation intentionally do to achieve this mission? The congregation's purpose is not only to strengthen the institution, but also to nurture its members to connect faith and daily life intentionally.

Intentionality is the key. A 1990 year-long study with more than thirty congregations in three Methodist annual conferences attempted "to explore how congregations empower people to live as Christian disciples and to examine the climate and leadership within congregations that help people live Christian lives in the home, workplace, and community."[3] One finding was that

> in many congregations, one's faithfulness is measured by loyalty to the programs and internal life of the congregation; hence, the issue of connecting faith to daily life is not given much attention or support. . . . many congregations leave the impression that moving faith into life arenas is either optional or left to each individual.[4]

Another finding was even more revealing:

> Leaders in the church tend to operate under the assumption that by strengthening the infrastructure of the congregation, people will be empowered to live as Christian disciples in the realms of daily life. Our study leads us to conclude that strengthening the infrastructure is just that: building up the internal life of the congregation. It does not lead people to connect faith to daily life.[5]

And perhaps the most crucial discovery was that

> many people report that they rarely talk about God in church. They talk about many other things, but have few moments to express their relationships with God. For some, church is the last place they would expect to talk about God.[6]

The temptation is immediately to recommend specific programs and activities for the congregation. Although these are important and this book suggests a number of them, the most crucial element to help members connect faith and daily life is to have this mission *permeate* every program and activity of the congregation. Rather than seeing ministry in daily life as a separate and isolated understanding, approach and evaluate and *connect* every aspect of congregational life with the question: How will this support members to be ambassadors for Christ in their daily lives? Does our worship lead to such a response? Is our educational program equipping people to be disciples? Does our understanding and practice of stewardship help people to see that their lives are the most important gift to be given back to God? Only by really probing such questions will the challenge of being a church in mission in the world become the *bloodstream* of the congregation. Then discipleship is not only serving the church but being in ministry as God's agents in God's world. The energies will be primarily devoted to the spiritual motivation of each member, to growing together in congregational life, and to making a difference in the outside world.

By connecting our faith more deeply and fully with each part of our daily living, we exemplify a life of faithful service as well as witness to the power of Christ and the guidance of the Spirit. Never underestimate how God works through each of us in where we are each day.

With diverse ministries—differing gifts and roles and places of service—all of us are called to the common task, as individual people and together, to serve our broken and disjointed world. We are called to connect!

### Reflection-Action-Reflection

1. Within a small group or with at least one other person, look once again at the words listed earlier in this chapter and again below.
2. Each person should choose from the list below one verb and intentionally attempt to connect people by acting on this verb. Set a time (perhaps one week from now) to come back together for mutual accountability.
   - *Relate* to two members of your family (immediate or extended) who are not communicating well together.
   - *Link* two people who may not know or understand one another's views on an issue.
   - *Intersect* with a person at your workplace who has seemed on "a different wavelength" from yours.
   - *Bridge* two committees or groups that are divided by a chasm of misunderstanding or real difference.
   - *Meet* two new members of your congregation and find a way for them to meet one another.
3. Use the following questions as guidelines for your discussion together before you go forth:

- What will be the challenge of connecting the people you are thinking about?
- What are ways of dealing with this difficulty?
- What may happen if you do not attempt to link these people?
- What are possible results if the people begin to connect with each other?

## CHAPTER 14

# Risking the Adventure

In my (Nelvin's) rural Minnesota village in the forties, one of the important events was the annual Summer Mission Fest, a time when missionaries talked about their work. It wasn't the talks that were eagerly anticipated; the food at the specially constructed wooden pavilions and the rollicking games kids played between and after the sessions made the occasion one of the high points of the summer. But of course all of us kids had to sit next to our parents during the speeches.

It may come as no surprise that I was not paying particular attention when a recent seminary graduate was introduced as a new missionary to Ceylon. But his first sentence startled me: "Thank you for giving me a thirteen-thousand-mile ticket to adventure!" Adventure and Christianity—how could they go together? Adventure is what happened in worlds of books and radio programs.

Adventure—to explore, to meet challenges, to overcome obstacles, to be excited about the future, to move boldly, to struggle against huge odds, and most of all, to be willing to take great risks—that really is our journey of faith, both as individual people and as communities of faith. Open to change, we travel and explore each day of our lives. We know God is present and trust that God cares about what we do each day. This trust frees us from depending totally on self, others, or institutions for security and allows us to risk for Christ's sake.

## Live by Faith

That kind of risk-filled living is what each person experienced as described in Hebrews 11, the chapter on the pantheon of the faithful. The litany "By faith. . . . By faith . . . " evokes witnesses who overcame obstacles, met challenges, and put their whole trust in God.

Each person's faith was formed and molded by the particular context of experience. Noah's faith was tested by the decision to build or not to build the ark, foolish as the action seemed. The faith of Abraham was absolutely changed by going on a journey, "not knowing where he was going." Sarah's faith grew out of the amazing birth she experienced when far past child-bearing years. And so with the rest of the saints of Hebrews 11. They put their confidence in God, but their faith was not something abstract. It was "the assurance of things hoped for"; it was "the conviction of things not seen" (v. 1). It was not merely a possible hypothesis; it was putting that conviction to the test. They struggled and wrestled with risky questions: Does it really make sense to build a big boat? Where are you sending me on this trip? Will a child actually come? They risked in their struggles of faith.

### Reflection

Recall three of your past actions that involved risk.

1.  What were your feelings about the unknown?
2.  How did you work your way through it?
3.  Do you see differences in each action or a pattern?
4.  What questions or dilemmas involving risk are you struggling with right now?
5.  How does your faith inform this struggle?
6.  To what is God calling you?
7.  What faithful people accompany you?

## Connect Faith and Daily Life

A Christian is one in whom God is keeping the struggle alive. A congregation is a community of faith in which God is keeping the struggle alive. Our theology, our thinking about God, grows out of our struggles. Our theology has its sources in particular events, in specific places and times, in the midst of ambiguity rather than clarity. The Gospel always comes in context, and it is always responded to in a particular time and place. That was the experience of David and Mary and Paul and Luther and Pope John XXIII and Martin Luther King and Mother Teresa. Faith and daily life interweave one with the other, sometimes confusing and difficult to figure out, but always an adventure of risk.

To connect, to really connect, faith and daily life is often difficult and full of risks—and so we avoid the connecting. The Middle Ages, for example, saw theology as the queen of the sciences, at the top of all knowledge—a hierarchical arrangement in which theology did not always interact with other human knowledge. A more modern version is to see theology or religion as the veneer, the lamination, the frosting, none of which has anything to do with the rest of life. Perhaps the most common approach is "the slice of life" perspective in which one's religion is simply another area of life, not to be mixed or related to any other part of one's experience. The tables of contents of *Time* and *Newsweek* exemplify this fragmentation. Such an approach is safe and entails little risk. Don't mix religion and politics, religion and business. Keep them safely separate. Make God limited to worship and prayer. Our day-to-day living —God can't be bothered by that.

But when Jesus was on earth, he was extremely interested in and concerned with people where they were in their daily lives: at a wedding, in their fishing, with their illnesses, in their relationships with one another.

God sanctified this world by sending Jesus to live and work among us. The world is charged with God's activity. The pity is that we often program ourselves to expect God to come to us only in our religious settings. God chooses instead to communicate with us in and through the people we are with—at the copy machine, in our homes, in parking lots, and even on tennis courts.

Such an understanding is much more difficult, but much more exciting, than to separate our faith and our daily life. It is to see one's faith in God as that which penetrates and integrates all of one's life. Our faith is not something added on or something extraneous, but that which unifies and makes sense of what is already taking place in our lives.

**Reflection**

1.  When have you been surprised by God's presence?
2.  To see God's presence in all of our living—what's adventurous *and* risky about that?

# To Minister Is To . . .

Nelvin sometimes opens up a discussion on faith and daily life by writing across the top of the blackboard:

> To minister is to _____.

Usually, the first response to that inquiry is "to serve." And then the various members of the group keep on adding:

> to respond
> to love
> to affirm
> to pray
> to teach
> to support
> to listen (we talk about Jesus in ministry who really listened to people)
> to be available
> to encourage
> to sing
> to challenge
> to worship
> to care for the Earth
> to witness
> to nurture

And the list goes on and on until the board is filled.

Then we ask: Were any of you involved in any of these actions last week? Will you be serving Christ in any of these ways next week? You have been in ministry; you will be serving as a minister, a priest, a disciple of Christ this coming week.

## Reflection

1. What other words would you add to the above list?
2. Were you involved in any of these actions last week?
3. Take some time mentally to walk through the past week and recall the varied experiences of ministry in which you were engaged.

Our ministry *in* daily life has at least five dimensions, each of which this book has described.

- Ministry *of:* All ministry is the response to Christ's love and finds its source in the ministry *of* Christ.
- Ministry *for:* We exist for the sake of others. We, like Christ, are to be the person *for* others.
- Ministry *with:* We are mutually interdependent and therefore all are in ministry *with* one another.
- Ministry *from:* Our service to Christ flows *from* our daily lives and is deeply rooted in our experiences.
- Ministry *into:* Our ministry moves *into* the world around us.

## To Minister Is Not To . . .

We should not forget that the call to ministry to each of us is not first of all what you and I do, but God working through us and in us and sometimes in spite of us. Ministry is not limited to certain people at certain times doing certain things.

Having affirmed that each of us is called, the impression may have been given that this means we should do more or be more, for example, do more for the church or be more tolerant. Although such actions may become part of the effects of the Spirit working within us, what must be emphasized is that our call is to serve where we are. Our calling comes through life experiences in our skills, interests, and opportunities that

God gives us. God seeks and finds and calls us where we are. God calls us into relationships and situations and out of them—out of certain areas of service and into another.

We are already in ministry. Ministry is not only something we go out and do. It is essentially something we do as we go. It takes place in the normal flow of events. We do not have to find our ministry; it finds us.

Ministry in daily life is like parenting; everybody's doing it, even though no one has been given a lot of instructions. Like parenting, we can hone our skills, deepen our insight, broaden our perspectives. Ministry in daily life is like breathing; it's natural and necessary for life as a Christian.

## A Congregation: Ministry with Mission

Four basic verbs describe how in the world a congregation can risk the adventure of ministry and strengthen its mission to be the body of Christ for others.

### To Recognize

It happens again and again! People suddenly recognize that the way they practice their occupations, the way they take care of an aged parent or communicate with a high school friend . . . may be ministry; it may be a response to God's love for us.

Such breakthroughs require places where Christians may share their faith and their fears. To recognize that God is in the so-called ordinary, that such activities are not neutral, opens up the vista of God already at work in our lives without our realizing it.

Pastors, church workers, and seminary students face the same challenges as all of us: to connect our faith and daily life within our personal relationships, our occupations, our leisure, and our involvement within the community. Religious leaders who recognize this tension within their lives are better able to serve and empathize with others.

## To Affirm

To affirm means more than to pat someone on the back to increase some-one's self-esteem. It involves a deep commitment that both motivates and makes constructive comments about another's journey. Affirmation may include identifying one's gifts and talents and abilities, strengthen-ing a pastor or a fellow worker who is weary and fatigued, listening at-tentively to someone else, or emphasizing that each of us is a bearer of the Gospel, both in the church and in the world.

All affirmation is in the spirit of the early Christians who kept on thanking God for others. Such statements make sense only because we need one another. God has placed us here to use our abilities to strength-en one another.

## To Equip

Each of us needs to be at the ready for whatever lies ahead. Therefore, appropriate preparation is prerequisite. The task is to equip one another so that we might serve as Christ's servants in the world. That implies that pastors and church leaders are to equip others for their ministry; they are not to do the work for others. Most of all, we are equipped by learning from one another within the Christian community.

When one congregation's adult forum decided to probe the implica-tion of health care, they did not turn exclusively to outside experts; they realized the group had within its membership health care professionals who could speak from first-hand experience. Such equipping of the saints, in the apostle's words, builds up the body of Christ.

## To Support

All that we've talked about amounts to nothing unless one experiences the support of God and others. Through celebration we are encouraged to continue, through financial support for training we are better equipped for our serving, and through small-group experiences we learn to share, to care, and to be aware of one another. Most of all, through regular prayer and study of the Scriptures, we are able to carry on.

*To recognize, to affirm, to equip,* and *to support*—these verbs describe how the church may nurture its members more intentionally to connect their faith and daily lives and challenge each of us to risk.

**Reflection**

1.  Describe how well your congregation
        recognizes
        affirms
        equips
        supports
    its members to connect faith and daily life.
2.  What other ways could your congregation strengthen you and the other members to risk connecting their faith and daily life?

## You and Your Mission

Did you ever go into an office whose purpose is to service customers and find all the employees talking to one another, busy with their own tasks, and no one coming to the counter to find out your need? We may not realize it, but this is too often a picture of the church in relation to the world. The only difference is that in the church, whoever does come to the counter will probably invite you to come inside, where some work will be found for you to do behind the counter.

That's not mission.

Mission is

- to have an urgent sense of being sent;
- to possess a drive and an urgency to be God's person and God's people in the world;
- to share the Good News always in all ways;
- to discern what God wants done in the world and then to do it with God.

## Risk the Adventure

You may have been tempted while reading this book to say, "That's all well and good, but people are busy. Who wants one more responsibility?" People seemingly prefer to remain mere audience in a worshipping congregation. But at a deeper level we hunger to be taken more seriously than that and to be held accountable for any commitments and values and actions. We want to be considered worthwhile and we want our lives to matter.

We may need to risk. No, make that we *need* to risk, no maybes about it. We need to risk doing that very thing people say they don't want to do. When we feel physically tired, instead of taking a nap, instead of indulging in a high-calorie treat, a brisk walk can often energize. Similarly, we need to start on the journey we believe we are too tired to finish. The risk holds within it the beginnings of new life.

Risk caring.

Risk being cared for.

Risk delegating.

Risk being called on.

Risk being called to task.

Risk being needed,

being needed more than once.

Risk learning more than you wanted to know;

"Sometimes I wish my eyes hadn't been opened."

Risk intervening.

Risk losing the battle.

Risk losing those you cared about and came to depend on.

Risk being disappointed.

Risk growing.

Risk the adventure.

Risk . . .

## Looking Back and Looking Ahead

As a child of God, you are called in your baptism.

No matter what your occupation or situation, you share in the ministry of Christ to the world.

As Christ's person, God keeps on calling you.

You are together in mission with other people of Christ.

You have been called to serve God in no other place and no other time than in the midst of the world in which you live.

Know this and give thanks. It is why you are here.

# NOTES

## Chapter 3
1. Judith Viorst, *Alexander and the Terrible, Horrible, No Good, Very Bad Day* (New York: Macmillan, 1972), np.

2. For a more full description of how a faith community can start a small group to equip one another for ministry, see Norma Cook Everist and Nelvin Vos, *Connections: Faith and World* (Chicago: Evangelical Lutheran Church in America, Division for Parish Services, 1986).

## Chapter 4
1. Marie Augusta Neal, "A Socio-Theology of Relinquishment," in *The Just Demands of the Poor* (New York: Paulist Press, 1987), 96ff.

## Chapter 5
1. Mitch Finley, "Confessions of a Modern Catholic Layman," *America* 166, no. 14 (April 22, 1989): 366.

## Chapter 7
1. Benny Hinn, *Welcome, Holy Spirit* (Nashville: Thomas Nelson, 1995), 121.

## Chapter 9
1. See Richard Hauser, *Moving in the Spirit: Becoming a Contemplative in Action* (Mahwah, N.J.: Paulist Press, 1986).

2. See Parker J. Palmer, *The Company of Strangers* (New York: Crossroad, 1981).

## Chapter 10
1. John Graff, reprinted by permission of the author.

## Chapter 11
1. Sören Kierkegaard, *Purity of Heart,* trans. Douglas V. Steere (New York:  Harper & Row, 1938), 163-64.
2. Elton Trueblood, *The Company of the Committed* (San Francisco: Harper & Row, 1961), 73-74.
3. Gregory Pierce, "No New Programs" (Speech delivered to the Task Force on the Study of Ministry of the Evangelical Lutheran Church in America, Chicago, October 1991). © 1991 by ACTA Publications, 4848 N. Clarke St., Chicago, IL 60640. Used by permission of the author.
4. Paul S. Minear, *Images of the Church in the New Testament* (Philadelphia:  Westminster Press, 1960).
5. H. Richard Niebuhr, *Christ and Culture* (New York:  Harper & Row, 1951), 1-44.
6. Richard J. Mouw, *Called to Holy Worldiness* (Philadelphia: Fortress Press, 1980).
7. George Carey, "Empowering the Priesthood of All Believers," *Trinity News* 39, no. 3: 11.

## Chapter 12
1. Celia A. Hahn, *Lay Voices in an Open Church* (Bethesda, Md.: The Alban Institute, 1985), 38.
2. Mark Gibbs, *Christians with Secular Power* (Philadelphia: Fortress Press, 1981), 37.

## Chapter 13
1. James H. Wolford, used by permission of the author.
2. Karl Barth (Lecture delivered at the University of Chicago, 1960).
3. Ray Sells, "Congregations and Connections:  Empowerment for Ministry," *Discipleship Dateline* 5 (May 1990): 1.
4. Ibid.
5. Ibid., 2.
6. Ibid.